Penguin Garden Centre Guides

Window Boxes and Pots

Martyn Rix

MAGNA BOOKS

This edition published 1992 by Magna Books, Magna Road,
Leicester, UK LE8 2ZH. Produced by the Promotional
Reprint Company Limited.

ISBN 1 85422 317 8

Edited and designed by Robert Ditchfield Ltd
Illustrated by Elaine Franks and Emma Tovey

Acknowledgements
The publishers would like to thank the following contributors and
copyright owners of the colour photographs:
Pat Brindley (4, 13, 36 above, 37 above, 48); Una and Denis Green (33
right); Diana Saville (9, 33 left, 36 below, 37 below, 60).

Printed & bound in Hong Kong

Contents

1. Introduction

Growing plants in containers appeals to two kinds of gardeners. For some, perhaps the majority, it is a necessity because they live in a flat and have no garden but only windowsills or sometimes a balcony or, if they are very lucky, a roof garden. For others, and they are increasing all the time, plants in containers are an interesting adjunct to a 'normal' garden: the containers emphasise some architectural feature, or enable tender plants to be grown outside in summer, and moved undercover away from frost in winter. Alpine plant enthusiasts, for example, grow some of their tiniest treasures in stone sinks where they are less likely to be lost, or pushed into oblivion by a frantic mole. And those who live on chalk or limestone soils may produce an acceptable environment for lime-hating plants such as dwarf rhododendrons or Himalayan gentians.

This book is for both kinds of gardeners. It is intended primarily for the beginner who wants to grow a wide range of plants in window boxes, pots and other containers. But it also includes ideas for unusual plants and interesting combinations and associations which will appeal to the experienced gardener and to those for whom containers are an adjunct to a large garden. (The growing of alpines is covered in more detail in the companion volume in this series.)

The preliminary pages deal with general topics such as the choice of containers readily available, how to prepare them for planting and where best to put them. This is followed by more detailed sections on the various types of plants which will grow

A window box serves the dual purpose of brightening the facade of a house as well as the view from within.

satisfactorily in containers (for example, annuals, shrubs, bulbs etc.) together with tables giving selections of suitable and easily obtainable varieties of each plant type, as well as their habit, flowering time, flower colour etc., so that you can plan a harmonious planting of several different plants in one container.

Towards the end there are some suggestions on which plants associate well together so that they both look good, and also grow satisfactorily when competing for both space and soil. If you make an unsuitable choice, one plant may completely swamp the other and the weaker one is killed.

There are sections on growing fruit and vegetables in containers, and a list of suitable varieties to look for. It is in this area that peat-filled polythene bags, sold by many companies (but by Fisons under the name Grobags) are useful. Many vegetables, for example tomatoes and peppers, do much better in them than if they are grown in the open ground. Most of them will thrive alongside flowers and many are ornamental in their own right.

No gardening is without its problems, but if watering and feeding are adequate, and the site is not too draughty, plants in window boxes and containers have fewer troubles than many other plants. Nonetheless, difficulties may occur, so one of the final sections discusses some of the pests and diseases which may cause problems, and suggests how to cure them. It is always best to deal with any disease or pest as soon as you spot it or suspect its presence, because most of them owe their success to their ability to breed quickly when they find conditions suitable. There is no better way than looking at your plants daily, so spotting and being able to rectify any problem of disease, lack of water etc. as soon as it shows itself.

Detailed instructions, to which it is very important to keep, are given on watering, feeding and general aftercare of the plants in the containers. It is care in these aspects that makes the difference between success and failure.

Fine terracotta pots with varied plantings make a handsome adornment to these curving brick steps.

2. Pots and Containers

There is such a wide range of materials, styles, sizes and shapes of container to choose from in almost every garden centre or shop, that it seems difficult at first to decide which to buy. The final choice will depend on the preference of the buyer and on the cost, but there are important differences in the characteristics of each container and the guidelines given here will help prevent an unsuitable choice which may be regretted later.

Size is important

The most suitable size for a container depends on the site and space available, and on the plants which the gardener wants to grow.

SMALL CONTAINERS The major drawback with small containers is that they require so much careful attention. Any container which will hold sufficient soil will grow plants. The smaller the size, the more attention it will need, because it will dry out more quickly and the goodness in the soil will be used up sooner. These two aspects are most important, indeed they are the commonest causes of failure; they are discussed in detail on pages 16–17. Some plants such as stonecrops and houseleeks grow naturally in small pockets of soil, and can survive frequent drying, but they are exceptions. Most plants soon die if they become completely dry, and both drought and too poor soil make them more liable to attack from pests. Small containers are safer in shady and sheltered places, protected from the drying effects of sun and wind.

LARGE CONTAINERS Very large containers have one major drawback – they are very difficult to move when planted up. It is often recommended that castors should be fixed onto wooden tubs and boxes, but large concrete, clay or fibreglass containers will need to be moved on rollers or on a specially made low platform. A collection should include a range of sizes to suit a variety of different plants which will provide colour and interest throughout the season. Fewer large pots are better than many small. On a formal terrace, however, a number of identical pots gives a better effect.

CONTAINERS FOR TREES AND SHRUBS As a general rule, the larger the plant, the larger the container. Shrubs and trees in particular (see pages 40–43) need reasonably deep pots or tubs if they are to make good growth. If the roots completely fill the container, the soil will dry out more quickly and watering will need to be more regular. Shrubs which have rather fleshy roots will survive drying better than those with very fine roots like rhododendrons. Hydrangeas, another popular subject, need plenty of water and feeding when growing to support their large leaves and flowerheads, and so will need plenty of rootroom. Formal evergreens, such as bay trees, which are meant to remain much the same size for years, will do in smaller containers.

CONTAINERS FOR OTHER PLANTS Perennials (pages 24–31) require rather deep containers, so that their leaves and flowers can develop properly, and the same is true for bedding plants and annuals (pages 18–23) if they are to make a good and long-lasting show. Early spring flowering bulbs (pages 44–49) such as crocus and dwarf iris will grow well in shallower pots and boxes; they associate well with dwarf annuals and drought-resistant alpines, all of which are adapted to withstand drying in summer.

Drainage

As well as being large enough to remain moist between waterings, all containers must have drainage holes in the bottom so that excess water can escape, and the soil does not remain saturated for long. Most containers meant for plants already have holes, but sometimes these will need enlarging if they are not to get blocked by soil. In addition you can put small crocks or pebbles at the bottom of the pot. If the drainage hole does get blocked, plants may die because the roots drown in the waterlogged soil.

Materials

When starting a collection of containers for a patio, balcony or terrace, it is better to choose a style which is appropriate to the setting. Plastic, concrete or modern materials suit a modern setting; terracotta looks best with brick or red sandstone, stone with stone of a similar colour. Wood is suitable every-where, either in its natural colour or painted to suit its surroundings. The fine fibre-glass imitations of lead period urns or tanks are appropriate for a period setting, and will be the nearest to the real thing that most people can afford. An interesting selection of contrasting shapes in one or two materials will look more attractive than a hotch-potch collection of different styles mixed together.

Plastic

Plastic is the most flexible material of which containers and pots are commonly made. It is also the cheapest and is available in the greatest variety of shapes and colours. It is light and very easy to move around when empty, in great contrast to concrete which is very heavy even before it is filled with soil. It is also impermeable to water, which means that plastic containers do not dry out as quickly as clay ones of the same size. Disadvantages are that it can be damaged quite easily and is not as long lasting as other materials, especially if it stands in the sun: and because it is thin and impermeable it does not have the effect of keeping the roots of the plants cool. There is also more danger of waterlogging in an impermeable container, a disadvantage shared by metal or glazed pottery.

A selection of plastic pots and containers is shown. White, black, and highly coloured ones are suitable for a modern setting, richly planted with brightly coloured geraniums, petunias or fuchsias. The dull green or terracotta coloured will pass in a traditional setting, or if planted with ferns, foliage plants or evergreens. They will be best in corners where it is awkward to water often. If you have a motley collection of differently coloured plastic pots, you will find that the actual containers will be almost invisible if you group small pots with spraying foliage in front of large pots.

Concrete

Concrete has many of the advantages of plastic. It is cheap, and can be mass-produced in a large variety of shapes. It is, however, very heavy. The largest pieces are usually made in two parts which fit together, but they still need careful moving even when empty. The great advantage of this weight is that boxes on walls, pedestals or gate-posts will not blow off and do not need careful fixing as do wooden ones. Concrete is porous to water, so that, unless the containers are very large, they will dry out in a relatively short time, especially if they are in an exposed or windy position. A lining of black polythene will slow the drying. It is important that the polythene should have drainage holes in it, and it need only reach just below the soil surface, so that it does not show. Concrete pots are unsuitable for growing lime-hating plants such as rhododendrons, since a certain amount of the lime in the concrete will seep into the compost.

A selection of concrete containers is shown. Most are imitations of stone and are in antique style, but modern designs are also commonly obtainable, and these are more appropriate in association with modern architecture. The imitations of old stone pots and urns are often made of coarser grained concrete so that they become coated with algae and lichen the sooner. The growth of green algae on the surface can be encouraged by spraying with liquid fertiliser and keeping the pot in the shade for a few weeks so that the surface remains moist. A special variation on a concrete container is the sink or trough made for alpine plants. Instructions on how to make this by covering a glazed sink with mock tufa are given on pages 32–33.

Reconstituted stone

Reconstituted stone is one of the most elegant, but unfortunately one of the most expensive of modern materials for containers. Several companies make excellent examples, based on original old designs which would have been carved out of solid stone. If these urns or basins are to be put in old gardens, they may look too new and need some encouragement to weather quickly. Painting with diluted cow manure, liquid fertilizer or even milk will encourage a green growth of algae to form, and tone down the colour of the new 'stone'.

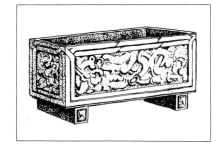

Fibre-glass

Fibre-glass has similar physical properties to plastic, but is stronger and more durable. It is used particularly for reproductions of fine antique urns, cisterns, tanks and vases. The finish may imitate either lead or stone; the lead is particularly effective. Recently imitations of wood have appeared, particularly Versailles boxes; they have the advantage over wood that they do not need frequent repainting or other measures to prevent rotting.

Wood

Wood is the commonest material for window boxes and square tubs for the formal planting of shrubs such as camellias and bay trees. Instructions for making and maintenance of window boxes are given on pages 12–13.

The commonest wooden containers are tubs, either specially made for plants or cut from old barrels. They are admirable for most plants as well as trees and shrubs as they hold enough soil without being too deep. They should be treated inside before planting so that the wood does not rot, either with a preserving fluid like Cuprinol (the special green type which is harmless to plants), or by burning the inside of the tub to produce a protective layer of charcoal. This can be done by lighting a fire of dry leaves or wood-shavings in the tub and letting it burn for a few minutes, until the inside is charred to a depth of about a fifth of an inch (5 mm). The layer of charcoal so formed is almost unrottable.

Wood swells when it is full of moisture, and you will find that if you allow a tub to dry out it will loosen up and the iron hoops may slip down. Guard against this by keeping it in constant use and moist. A few discreet nails below the hoops will prevent them slipping. Unpainted the tubs are suitable for an informal setting; painted all white or with the iron hoops contrasting in black, they are appropriate in a formal setting in town.

Terracotta

Terracotta is the traditional material for clay flower pots, but pots are now usually made of plastic. At the same time all sorts of interesting shapes have become available in terracotta, mostly imported from Italy. Because it is usually unglazed and porous, drying out can be a problem especially in summer, and in exposed windy sites in dry weather. At the same time this evaporation keeps the roots cool. Drying out can be reduced by lining part of a large container with polythene, and by standing the pots in a saucer in summer. These saucers can usually be bought to fit even the largest pots.

As terracotta is similar in colour to brick, it looks well associated with brick or warm coloured stone. It is available as window boxes, urns, amphorae (two-handled vessels in ancient, classical style), wall pots, herbs and strawberry pots as well as the usual flower pots. A selection is shown here.

Other materials for containers

The traditional materials, stone and lead, are now rarely used as they have become very expensive, but examples can still be bought more cheaply by those lucky enough to spot them in old junk heaps or country farm-yards. Old stone sinks are ideal for alpines, but if you cannot find the genuine article you will see how to make good imitations on pages 32–33; lead tanks are better for bedding plants. Fine examples of both these can be seen in many famous gardens.

Many other old objects can make fine containers. Wooden wheel-barrows make attractive stands in which to place groups of pots, or they can be lined with polythene and planted. They have the advantage of being easily movable. Old casseroles or saucepans are good if drainage holes can be bored in them. Plastic yoghurt cartons make excellent small pots, and larger containers can be made from cracked washing-up bowls, and family-size ice-cream cartons. Drainage holes are easily made in them with a hot poker.

Hanging Baskets

Hanging baskets are usually made of strong wire, but plastic, such as is used for salad shakers, would also be suitable though less durable. The soil is kept in place by lining the inside of the basket with moss. This both holds water and prevents the soil drying out too quickly. If moss is not easily obtainable, black polythene makes an adequate substitute. Watering should be very regular and copious, so the basket must be hung where it is reasonably accessible. The plants should be grown almost to flowering size before the basket is hung up; meanwhile it can stand on an empty flower pot.

Most hanging or trailing plants are suitable for baskets; the trailing varieties of lobelia, ivy-leafed geraniums, pendulous tuberous begonias, fuchsias and petunia are among the most satisfactory. Ivies are suitable for permanent planting.

An elegant terracotta tub standing on stone flags at the corner of a lawn, planted with contrasting flowering and foliage plants: *Petunia* 'Purple Defiance' and *Helichrysum* 'Limelight'.

3. Preparation and Soil

The quality and fertility of the soil in a container is absolutely fundamental to the success of the plants growing in it, and so it is worth extra care and expense.

Drainage

Few plants will survive for any length of time with their roots in completely waterlogged soil. The roots need air, or at least oxygen, and will soon die if they are drowned; furthermore, the soil becomes 'sour', and the texture and fertility are lost.

To prevent waterlogging in wet weather, or after very generous watering, all containers should have a hole in the bottom, large enough not to get blocked too easily. To prevent blockage, a piece of broken pot or a large stone should be placed over the hole.

To assist free drainage, a layer of coarse gravel or old bricks is usually placed over the bottom of the container; this need not be very deep – about 1 inch (2.5 cm) is ample. To prevent the gravel layer becoming blocked by soil, a layer of peat is often put on top of the gravel. This also acts as a sponge to retain water and the plant roots will be found growing thickly in this layer. Where peat composts are being used, the peat layer will, of course, be quite unnecessary. Pots, window boxes and the smaller containers should be stood on trays or saucers, as described on page 17 under the heading of watering. These also help to prevent worms entering the container and causing the soil to become compacted.

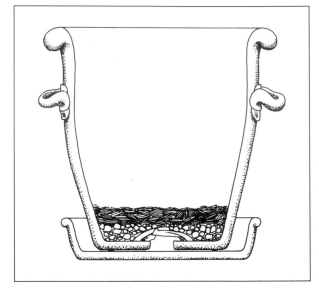

Cross section of pot showing drainage in place, with gravel and a peat layer above it to prevent the drainage from becoming blocked.

Peat composts

Two main sorts of peat-based, soil-less composts are commonly available; one, such as Levington, without sand, the other, such as Arthur Bower's, with sand added to assist drainage.

Plants grow very well in peat compost, but because the peat itself has no nutrients in it, regular feeding is essential if the plants are to thrive for any length of time. (There should be some indication on the bag as to how soon nutrients in the form of the liquid fertilizers, mentioned under 'Feeding' on page 17, will need to be applied.) Peat has a further disadvantage in that once it has dried out, which it does more slowly than soil-based composts, it is very difficult to re-wet. It is therefore better to use it only in plastic pots or window boxes, or in areas where there is little risk of drying.

For these two reasons peat compost is most suitable for annuals and short-lived plants which will be discarded or removed at the end of the summer. Plantings of shrubs or climbers, which have to last more than one year are best made in a soil-based compost such as John Innes (see below).

'Grow-bags' or other peat-filled polythene bags designed for growing plants are especially excellent

A peat-filled polythene bag or 'Grow-bag', excellent for growing warmth-loving vegetables such as tomatoes, aubergines and peppers. Nutrients are added to the peat, sufficient for the first month or so of plant growth; after that regular feeding is vital.

for vegetables such as tomatoes, peppers etc., and are covered in more detail under the heading 'Vegetables' on page 54.

Soil composts

In the past each gardener had his own favourite mixture of loam, sand or grit and peat or leaf-mould for growing different plants. Then experiments at the John Innes Institute showed that most plants grew perfectly well in one standard mixture, and this became known as John Innes potting compost: it consists of seven parts of loam, to two parts of coarse sand or fine grit, and three parts of peat, to which is added ground chalk and a mixed, rather slow-release fertilizer. The numbering of the compost (John Innes No. 1, 2 or 3) merely denotes the amount of fertilizer added.

The quality of the mixture depends greatly on the quality of the ingredients, but generally the mixtures sold in large bags are good enough, although they can usually be improved by the addition of a further quarter or so of peat.

Composts such as John Innes are best for long-term planting, for shrubs and for use in terracotta pots and containers made of porous material. Some plants, notably box or yew bushes, and most herbs are probably the better for the addition of extra chalk.

Lime-hating plants, such as rhododendrons, azaleas, camellias and heathers need lime-free soil, and for these J. Arthur Bower's Ericaceous Mixture will be suitable. For a longer useful life this compost may be mixed with coarse lime-free sand or with John Innes seed compost which should contain less chalk. Take care not to water lime-haters with alkaline tap water – an easy test is whether the water causes your electric kettle to fur up or turns red cabbage bluish. If you suspect your tap water is alkaline, use rain water or weak tea (cold!) to keep these lime-haters healthy.

A camellia in a pot. It is very important that the roots of all camellias (and other slightly tender shrubs such as bays) are protected from frost either by being taken indoors in really cold weather, or by surrounding the pots with straw or old newspapers kept dry with a polythene dustbin bag.

Filling the container

When the drainage and peat layers are in place, and a suitable compost has been selected, the container, be it pot, window box or large tub, can be filled to within 2 to 4 in (5–10 cm) of its rim, depending on its size and the bulk of the plants to be put in it. For example, if spring bulbs are to go in, or seed, you will need more soil than if you are planting a group of already potted plants, such as pelargoniums.

The compost should be gently pressed down, or left for a day or so to settle before planting. Always make sure that there is a gap of at least $1\frac{1}{2}$ to 3 in (3.7–7.5 cm) at the top of the pot so that it can be watered properly. Err on the generous side with this gap; it is easier to add a little more soil, than to dig out the extra from among already growing plants.

If the plants to be grown are going to need staking, (for example, if lilies are being planted), it is advisable to put in the stakes or supports when the container is filled and before planting is done.

A pot filled showing the correct depth left for easy watering. After a year permanently planted specimens such as shrubs should have the top couple of inches of soil removed and replaced with fresh compost into which some fertilizer has been mixed.

4. Window Boxes

A window box may be the nearest thing to a garden that many flat-dwellers can manage. Fortunately most plants will do well in window boxes, provided that they are neither exceptionally exposed to wind nor completely shaded. They can be full of flowers or even grow fruit such as strawberries, or many different vegetables.

As with all containers, drying out in windy weather is the major problem. The first essential therefore, is to have the window box as large as possible, in depth, width and length. A depth and width of 8 in (20 cm) is the smallest which is likely to be successful for any plants except those that are really drought-resistant, or can be watered every day in dry weather.

Different materials have been mentioned on pages 7–9. Window boxes are to be had in most of them, but wood is especially suitable, even though it needs cleaning and repainting regularly if it is to last.

If the window ledge is too narrow to support such a large box safely, or if the windows need to be opened outwards, the box may be suspended on brackets, so that its top is level with the sill. This has the advantage that the back of the box is not seen from inside the house. Suitable brackets may be bought with some boxes, but they are not difficult to make. Ideally they should allow the box to rest securely in them, but permanent boxes may be screwed to their supports, if they are to be filled with another box or pots, and will not need to be moved.

Making your own box

It is not difficult to make your own wooden window box, and it has the advantage that it can be designed to fit the window. It may be filled directly with compost, but there is no doubt that it will last longer if it is used only as an outer box, and the plants are grown in a plastic box placed inside the wooden one.

The window box can be made of any timber, but it should be about $\frac{1}{2}$ in (1.2 cm) thick; marine ply offcuts which can sometimes be had cheap, are ideal. If you are skilled in carpentry, you can make the corners with dove-tail joints; if not the corners can be screwed and glued, as in the diagram, and perhaps strengthened with corner pieces inside. Cut the corner pieces lower than the rim of the box so that a plastic box will fit inside the wooden one and not be held up by its lip.

After assembly, paint the box well – two coats of primer, followed by undercoat and a weather-resistant surface paint in the desired colour. If a wood finish is wanted a good exterior varnish should be used. Be sure to paint both the inside and the outside of the box, and the joints and corners.

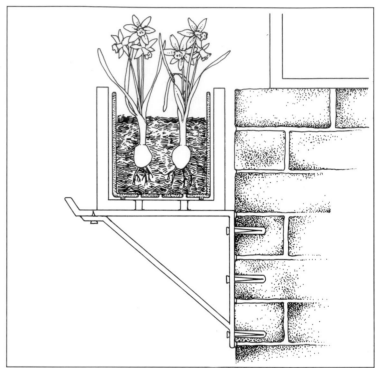

One way to position window boxes is with strong metal brackets fixed securely to the wall below the window ledge.

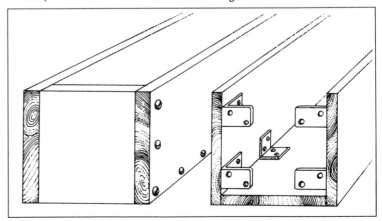

Two simple methods of constructing a wooden window box. You can drill and screw directly into thicker wood, but brackets of some kind are needed for thinner wood.

Planting and after-care

If the plants are grown in separate small containers, they can simply be plunged in the window box, and the pots hidden by peat or bark chippings. If the pots are plastic, it will matter little whether the peat be wet or dry, but if clay pots are used, wet peat will be better to keep the pots moist.

When the plants are going to be grown directly in the box, it should be put into position before it becomes too heavy to lift. The final planting can be done when the box is in position, and when planted it will probably not be easy to move. Filling and planting will be the same as for other containers, but only enough drainage need be put along the base to keep the holes from becoming blocked.

Ample water is vital for window boxes which are nearly always in a draughty position. Once a week, except in winter, is a minimum, and daily waterings may be needed in warm dry weather in spring and summer. Feeding weekly with Tomorite or some other balanced fertilizer is also beneficial once flowering has begun. Remember that most window boxes are overhung by the eaves or window ledge above, and receive very little rain, so they need watering even in wet weather.

If the window boxes are particularly exposed to sun and wind, the usual plants such as petunias and *Impatiens* and lobelias will not grow well. They may have a few flowers but will soon deteriorate in hot weather. Plants which originate in drier climates will survive better. Geraniums (*Pelargonium*) are good; they will not die if they get dry for a day or two, and although one lot of flowers may wither, new ones will soon come out when watering resumes. The orange *Mimulus glutinosus* survives drought, as do the various blue Cape Daisies (*Felicia bergeriana* and other species), and red, orange or yellow gazanias. Here many herbs will thrive; thymes, rosemary, sage and oregano are all drought resistant and will grow in the sunnier places. Many alpines will also do well, their native habitat being dry rock ledges, with little soil; *Sempervivum* species, *Saxifraga cochlearis*, *Potentilla nitida*, *Draba aizoides*, and *Origanum amanum* will all survive in such places.

Pelargoniums are excellent subjects for a sunny window box as they will survive a day or two without water.

5. Choosing Plants, Planting and After-care

When buying plants for your containers, take care to buy only those which are strong-growing and bushy. Take particular care not to buy those bedding plants offered for sale too early in the year. They may be weak and spindly, and will probably succumb to late frost. Mid-May is quite early enough to plant out most bedding plants, and some such as heliotrope are better left until early June when all danger of frost is past.

Make sure that the plants are not overcrowded in their boxes when you buy them, and that they have been hardened off sufficiently; the leaves should be dark and healthy looking. Avoid unhealthy plants with yellowing leaves or those that look diseased, and try to resist the temptation of buying plants, especially annuals, which are already in flower; they are likely to have been starved and will never make large floriferous plants.

Perennials such as pelargoniums, dahlias or begonias are best when grown in individual containers, and it is worth paying the extra price for these, as they will make much larger plants in the long run and make a better show.

Planting

Having prepared your containers as described on page 11, you are now ready to plant them up.

1. The first stage is to soak the plants in their present pots and boxes before you place them in their new containers. If you plant them out when they are dry, there is a danger that the soil around their roots will remain dry, even when the compost around them has been wetted.

2. Next, take a trowel and dig out a hole in the compost-filled container, which is sufficiently large to accommodate the roots of the plant comfortably. Do not try to cram these roots into too small a hole.

3. Fill in the hole, shaking the plants gently to make sure that the compost is all round the roots, and press the soil firmly round the plant so that it is perfectly firm and will not rock about in any wind. Keep the plants at the same level as they were in their boxes or pots; if you bury them too deeply in the soil they may rot.

4. When you have finished planting, water the plants thoroughly to settle them in, using a fine rose on your watering-can. Finally, you can cover the surface of the compost with pebbles or small stones; these give a tidy appearance and also help to conserve moisture in the soil, as will a layer of moist peat or bark. In addition, the covering will serve to prevent splashing of the soil in heavy rain.

Arranging plants

The number of plants and how to arrange them depends very much on the size and shape of your container. Try and achieve an informal effect and avoid straight rows and blobby effects. In a window box, place tall plants at the back, with shorter ones in the front and at the sides, with trailing plants hanging over the front. It must be remembered, however, that a window box can often be seen from inside the house as well as from outside, and this must be taken into account when arranging your plants.

One way of achieving a succession of colour in containers is to fill them with a moist, peaty compost and plunge the plants into this in their pots, so that they can be removed and replaced by others as they fade. An alternative idea is to have a removable lining which can be extracted with the plants and replaced by another of the same size, already planted for the next season.

A third system is to have enough containers so that they can be brought out as their floral contents come to maturity, to replace those that are fading. This is especially feasible if a frost-free greenhouse is available, so that the more tender plants can overwinter inside and be brought out in the summer months.

Tulips, daffodils and other bulbs tend to look very unsightly when the foliage is dying down. Either move the containers out of view, or lift the bulbs with the foliage intact and lay them or plant them out in the garden so that the foliage can die down naturally.

Maintain a succession of flowers in a box or large container by regularly replacing small pots in the compost.

An alternative is to prepare a series of inner containers planted for each season.

Dead-heading and other after-care

Cutting off all dead flower heads before they set seed will keep your plants flowering much longer, and this, together with weeding and removing any dying foliage, should be carried out regularly. Plants vary in their response to dead-heading. Some, such as sweet peas, will stop flowering very quickly if they are allowed to set their seed pods; others, such as petunias, will keep flowering as long as they are well fed and watered.

Staking

Taller plants growing in containers may have to be staked, especially if they are in an exposed position. Make sure that the stakes are as unobtrusive as possible, and use green canes or bushy twigs to support the plants in a natural position.

6. Watering and Feeding

Plants will only thrive in containers and achieve their maximum potential if you water and feed them well and reliably. It is no good planting up your tubs and window boxes at the end of May, admiring your handiwork, and then deserting them for a prolonged holiday! The result will be a waste of plants and of your time.

When and how to water

Give the compost in your containers a thorough soaking, and allow the excess water to drain away before planting. Thereafter watering should be carried out regularly – this means once or twice a DAY during the summer, in sunny or windy weather, depending upon the size of the pot and the plant it contains. A large plant in a small pot will obviously need watering more often than a small plant in a large pot. The situation of the pot must also be taken into consideration; containers in full sunshine need to be watered more frequently than those standing in the shade.

The best time to water is in the evening so that the plants will have the benefit of the moisture all night before the drying sun is on them again. Even in the winter a watch should be kept on all plants in containers, as they can still get very dry, especially if they are standing under an overhanging roof.

There is a right and a wrong way to water plants.

Try and use rainwater that has been standing in a tank rather than water from the tap. Rainwater is free from lime which some plants, such as rhododendrons and azaleas, may dislike, and is also less cold than tap-water. It is rather unkind to soak your plants with ice-cold water on a summer's day, so if no rainwater supply is available, fill your can after finishing your watering and leave it to stand in the sun so that the water will lose its chill. Avoid directing a powerful jet of water from the hose-pipe or can on to your pots; you will merely wash the soil out of the containers, damage the plants, or at least spoil the look of them by splashing them with mud.

Be careful not to overwater in cold wet weather or the plants will flop and die because the roots are drowned in waterlogged soil. Make sure that the saucers the pots are standing in are not full of rain for more than a day or two.

It may be necessary to water window boxes and hanging baskets with a hose from the top of a ladder if they cannot be soaked adequately from within the house.

Hanging baskets

Hanging baskets present a special problem, and it is best to consider this when siting your baskets so that it is not impossible to reach them with a can. Peat mixed with the compost helps to retain water, but because of their size and the number of plants grown in them, hanging baskets tend to dry out very quickly. If the compost becomes too dry, it can form a crust on the surface, so that, when it is watered, most of the water will either run out of the side of the basket or simply fall straight on the head of anyone unfortunate enough to be standing below!

The method is to water gently and frequently so that plants never flag. It may be worth trying the old trick of placing a saucer at the bottom of the basket to catch some of the water as it trickles through, and some gardeners line their baskets with polythene to retain moisture. This doesn't look very ornamental, especially when the plants are small, and the use of sphagnum moss is preferable, as it remains green and acts as a sponge.

Holidays

For those who have unavoidably to leave their containers for any length of time, there are various watering systems on the market to do the job for them. A trip to the nearest garden centre or garden shop will show what is available. A cheaper method which works well is to remove all your containers into the shade and to pack them into deep trays of very wet peat, or to place each container in a washing-up bowl of water; these should keep the plants damp for two or three weeks – not very aesthetic perhaps, but you won't be there to see it.

In dry summers, and if for any reason you are unable to water your plants daily, it is a great help to have the plant pots standing permanently in terracotta saucers, shallow dishes made of the same material as the pots, but without drainage holes. These are very useful because they catch much of the water which runs through when the plant is watered, and ensure that the compost is well soaked every time. In winter or wet weather these saucers must be reversed so that the pots do not become waterlogged. The larger the saucer is than the pot which it contains, the more water it will hold, so plants which need wetter soil should have extra large saucers.

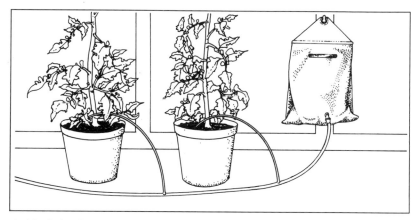

A drip-irrigation system, taking its supply from either a tank or directly from a tap, will keep pots constantly watered.

Plunge your pots into a large box containing very wet peat if you are going away.

Feeding

Assuming that you have used a good compost (see page 10) in your containers, there will be no need to start feeding your plants until they have become well established, normally about a month after planting. They should then be given a liquid feed, such as Maxicrop, Phostrogen or some other proprietary brand, at fortnightly intervals for the first month, and thereafter weekly, always making sure that the compost is moist before giving the feed.

Permanent plants such as shrubs need to have compost scraped from the surface each spring, before being top-dressed with fresh compost. If a plant is in a small container, it also needs liquid feeding while it is in active growth in early summer.

7. Annuals

The majority of plants which you will grow in your containers and window boxes to give a colourful display in the summer months will be those known as annuals, which is the name given to a plant which is sown, blooms and dies in one year. Most summer bedding plants are annuals. A biennial (see pages 22–23) must be sown one year to bloom in the following year, so they are usually bought as young plants in autumn.

Raising plants

By far the cheapest way to obtain plants for your containers is to raise your own. Not everyone has a greenhouse or frame, but a warm window-sill is quite sufficient for many plants; or one of the small, heated mini-propagators now on the market could be purchased. There are several different makes and you could compare them at your garden centre or nursery. For growing on and hardening off your plants, you can use cloches. Either make these at home, from sheet plastic which can be supported with wire or bent canes, or you can simply buy the glass or plastic cloches that are available.

Half-hardy annuals such as petunias, lobelias, pot marigolds, *Impatiens* and *Phlox drummondii* can all be raised in this way, and there are many others. Over the page you will find a list of plants to help you make a choice and this can be supplemented from a good seed catalogue.

The seed needs to be sown in late February or early March to make good plants for the summer. Using a good seed compost such as John Innes or Levingtons, which can be obtained ready-mixed in bags from your garden shop or nursery, fill boxes or pots with drainage holes, to within about ½ inch (1.2 cm) from the top with slightly damp compost; give the box a shake to level the compost, and firm the surface with a suitable piece of wood. Sow the seeds as thinly as possible, cover with a thin layer of sieved compost, and place a sheet of glass and a piece of paper over the container and leave in a warm position or in your heated propagator until germination takes place. Remove the covering immediately the seedlings appear and, as soon as they are large enough to handle, prick them out in boxes of John Innes No. 1 or Levingtons compost, spacing 2–2½ in (5–6.2 cm) apart according to their size, or prick out into individual pots. The Jiffy peat pots are useful as the plant can be put into its flowering position in its pot without disturbing the roots.

Plants must be hardened off by being placed in a cold frame, or stood outside and covered with a cloche at night, for two or three weeks until they are ready to be planted into their containers.

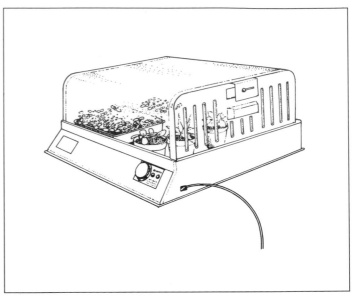

A small heated mini-propagator is invaluable for raising plants.

One of the many kinds of cloche that are available for hardening off plants before they are placed outside.

Choosing your annuals

While all the annuals mentioned in the table overleaf will grow successfully in pots, window boxes or other containers, a few are particularly satisfactory because of the ease with which they grow and their long flowering season.

For sunny positions, that is those which have full sun for three hours or more each day, **petunias** are especially good. Their flowers are quite long-lasting and sweetly, if faintly, scented. If well fed and watered, they will continue flowering throughout the summer. Their flowers come in all colours from purple to red, magenta, pink, white, and pale yellow; there are also double and striped forms. They are loose in habit and cover the edges of containers in an attractive way.

In sites which are even sunnier and hotter, **Californian poppies** (*Eschscholzia*) are very good. Each flower lasts only a day, but the plants continue to flower all summer, and will stand drought well. Orange is the usual colour, but there is an attractive strain now available with flowers in different shades of pink.

The best trailing annuals are the **lobelias**. In fact they are perennials in areas with mild winters, but are usually grown as annuals and young plants make a better show. The pale trailing forms make the most attractive plants, and care should be taken not to get the compact dark blue or purple-flowered forms which are suitable only for formal bedding.

For positions in half-sun or semi-shade **Lavatera trimestris** is very suitable. It can be sown where it is to flower, but makes a better plant (about the size of a small shrub with large hibiscus-like flowers) if grown singly in a large container in rich soil. The form 'Silver Cup' is a beautiful pink with silver lines, while 'Mont Blanc' is an exceptionally pure white.

Totally shady patios are often a problem in large towns and little will grow in them, but a few, such as **Begonia semperflorens** and **Impatiens** will survive and flower well in this environment. The best is *Impatiens sultani*, the Busy Lizzie, and its hybrids, formerly much grown as a sickly window-sill plant, but now more often seen as a very colourful and floriferous annual. Flowers come in intense shades of red, pink and magenta, with pale pinks and whites also available. They can be bought in spring as young plants, or seed can be sown indoors in March and planted out in May or early June.

Eschscholzia

Lavatera trimestris

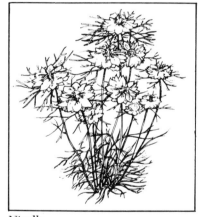

Nigella

Mesembryanthemum

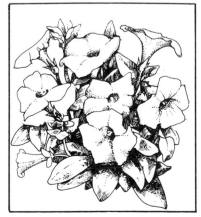

Petunia

Pot Marigold

List of annuals

The following plants will flower from seed sown outdoors, so can be sown direct into containers standing outside. Seed of many of the plants listed can also be sown in September for flowering the next summer. Heights vary according to the strain, compost, amount of water etc, but those given as low will grow up to about 6 in (15 cm), short about 6–9 in (15–23 cm), medium 1–2 ft (30–60 cm) and tall up to about 3 ft (90 cm). Botanical names are given in parentheses.

Name of plant	Colour of flower. Habit of plant.	When to sow	Flowering period
Alyssum (*A. maritimum*)	White or purple. Low, bushy growth.	March–April	June–September
Candytuft (*Iberis amara*)	White, pink, or purple shades. Short, upright growth.	March–May	July–September
Chrysanthemum (*C. carinatum, C. coronarium*)	White, yellow, orange, red. Erect, medium height.	April–June	July–September
Clarkia (*C. elegans*)	White, pink, lilac etc. Bushy, medium height.	March–May	July–September
Convolvulus (*C. tricolor*)	Blue with cream centre. Erect, bushy growth.	April	July–September
Cornflower (*Centaurea cyanus*)	Blue, white, pink, red, purple. Erect, bushy growth.	March–May	June–September
Eschscholzia (*E. californica*)	Orange – yellow, or pink shades. Spreading, medium height.	March	June–October
Godetia (*G. grandiflora*)	White, pink, lilac, red shades. Compact, bushy plant. Medium height.	March–April	June–August
Larkspur (*Delphinium ajacis*)	Blue or violet. Tall, upright.	March–April	June–August
Lavatera (*L. trimestris*) 'Silver Pink', 'Mont Blanc'	Pink or white. Bushy, tall.	April	July–September
Limnanthes (*L. douglasii*)	White, with yellow centre. Low, spreading.	March	June–August
Love-in-a-mist (*Nigella damascena*)	Blue, purple, pink, white. Upright, medium.	March	June–August
Lupin (*Lupinus hartwegii*)	White, blue, pink shades. Tall, bushy growth.	March	July–October
Marigold, pot (*Calendula officinalis*)	Yellow, orange. Bushy, medium height.	March	May–September
Nasturtium (*Tropaeolum majus*) – dwarf, bushy forms	Yellow, orange, red. Trailing stems.	April	June–September
Nemophila (*N. menziesii*)	Blue, with white centre. Low-growing, spreading habit.	March	June–August
Poppy (*Papaver rhoeas*)	White, pink, red. Upright, medium height.	March–April	June–August
Stock, night-scented (*Matthiola bicornis*)	Lilac (not spectacular; this plant is grown for its strong scent). Bushy, medium height.	April	July–August
Stock, Virginian (*Malcolmia maritima*)	White, pink, red shades. Low-growing.	March–July	April–August
Sunflower (*Helianthus annuus*)	Shades of yellow. This plant can grow up to 10 ft (3 m) in height!	March–April	July–September
Toadflax (*Linaria maroccana*)	White, pink, yellow and red shades. Slender, upright, low-growing.	March–April	June–July

Impatiens sultani is one of the most reliable and colourful of summer-flowering annuals.

Half-hardy annuals

All the plants listed below must be started off in the warm, so sow seed under glass or indoors.

Name of plant	Colour of flower. Habit of plant.	When to sow	Flowering period
Begonia semperflorens	White, pink or red. Short, bushy plants.	March–May	July–September
Impatiens balsamina and *I. sultani* hybrids (Busy Lizzie)	White, pink, red and purple shades. Bushy, medium height.	March–April	June–September
Lobelia (*L. erinus*)	Blue, white, purple. Trailing or low-growing bushy forms are available.	March–May	June–October
Mesembryanthemum (Ice plant)	Orange, pink, white or mauve. Shining, daisy-like flowers. Low, trailing.	March–May	July–September
Petunia (*P. hybrida*)	White, pale yellow, red, purple and pink. Very floriferous. Low, spreading or hanging.	March–May	June–September
Phlox drummondii	White, pink, red and purple. Bushy plant, dwarf to medium (according to variety).	March–May	July–September
Venidium (*V. fastuosum*)	Orange, with black centre. Tall.	May	June–October

8. Biennials

Biennials are, strictly speaking, plants which are sown one year and flower the next, whereupon they set seed and die. They are valuable because they make most of their growth in late summer and early autumn, and so can produce a good show of flowers earlier than can annuals. They are especially valuable in areas which have dry summers and mild wet winters, such as are found in the south of France and Spain bordering the sea. Some plants such as wallflowers will only behave as biennials, and are not likely to flower the same year even if planted early enough. They may however survive for a second flowering, and so behave as short lived-perennials. Others such as sweet peas and cornflowers may behave as biennials if sown late one year to flower the following spring, but will act as annuals if planted in spring.

Most of the plants mentioned in this section have been cultivated for many years, and several different varieties are available from seed. Those of compact habit will be more suitable if the containers in which they are to be grown are in a windy site. Taller ones will give a more informal effect, but will need more space and shelter.

Seed of biennials should be sown from early to late summer, according to variety, in boxes or in shallow drills in the open garden, and treated much as annuals. As soon as the plants are large enough to handle, plant them out into nursery lines (the plants 6–9 in (15–23 cm) apart), or prick them out into boxes. They should be fed and watered carefully, and the aim should be to produce strong bushy plants. If fed and watered too well, they may become too lush and weak, and therefore more susceptible to rotting and dying off in the winter.

It is best to plant biennials into the window boxes or pots in which they are to flower in late autumn, after the summer flowers have been thrown out. They then have the winter to get well established before the drier weather of spring. Remember again that all containers tend to dry out in windy weather, and this is even true of dry cold days in March and April. They may need watering at this time if they are to give the best possible display.

If you haven't the room or can't be bothered to raise the young plants yourself, you can often buy them from a garden centre or nursery in the autumn, ready for planting. Be sure to choose dark green, bushy plants and avoid those which are pale-looking or spindly, with dead leaves around the base. Wallflowers especially should be short and have many branches at the base of the main shoot.

Name	Flower colour, season and average height	When to sow seed	Notes
Brompton stock (*Matthiola*)	Purple to pink. May. 2 ft (60 cm).	August to September	Very sweet-scented flowers in spring, earlier than other stocks.
Canterbury Bell (*Campanula medium*)	Blue, pink or white. June. 1½ ft (45 cm).	June to July	Dwarf bedding varieties are the most suitable for containers.
Campanula incurva	Pale blue. July. 9 in but 2 ft spread (23 × 60 cm).	August	Like a creeping Canterbury Bell. Spectacular in flower.
Cornflower (*Centaurea cyanus*)	Blue to pink or purple. May to July. 1½ ft (45 cm).	September	Autumn-sown plants are usually larger and flower earlier than spring-sown ones.
Forget-me-not (*Myosotis*)	Blue, white or pink. April to May. 9 in (23 cm).	June	A good foil for tulips and other late spring bulbs.
Foxglove (*Digitalis*)	White or pinkish-mauve to peach colour. May to June. 3–6 ft (90–180 cm).	July	Ordinary foxgloves can be kept short by cutting out the central shoot below the flower buds.
Humea elegans	Green. June to July. 3–4 ft (90–120 cm).	July	Tall and incense-scented, with elegant drooping branches. Has been known to cause a rash to sensitive skins.
Iceland Poppy (*Papaver nudicaule*)	Orange to yellow, rarely pink or white. May onwards. 1½ ft (45 cm).	August to September	Needs well-drained but moist soil in sunny site. Good for picking.
Love-in-a-mist (*Nigella*)	Blue, purple or white. June to August. 1 ft (30 cm).	September	Autumn-sown plants are larger than spring-sown ones.
Wallflowers (*Cheiranthus*)	Yellow, orange, pink, red or purple. April to May. 1 ft (30 cm).	May to June	Very fragrant flowers; needs chalky soil, and good drainage.

Brompton stocks form branching plants which flower with great freedom in a wide range of colours including white, lilac, purple, pink and carmine. They are always grown as biennials, but in a light soil and mild area live for several years and still flower prolifically.

The Canterbury Bell, a favourite old-fashioned cottage plant, will produce large spires in early summer covered with its cup-and-saucer flowers of white, pink or blue. The tall varieties, which reach 3–4 ft (90–120 cm), are less suitable for growing in containers than the dwarf.

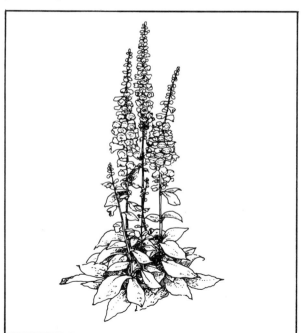

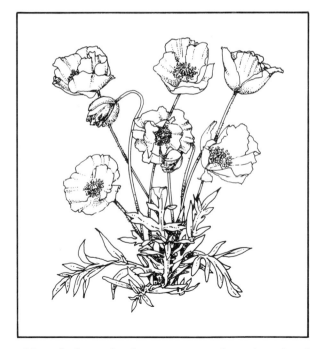

A large range of foxgloves can be grown from seed. Heights and colours vary, but good biennials include *Digitalis purpurea* 'Alba', a most beautiful white form growing to 4 ft (1.2 m) and *D.p.* 'Excelsior hybrids' up to 5 ft (1.5 m) with large flowers of cream, pink, carmine or purple. Both flower in summer.

Although the Iceland Poppy is strictly a short-lived perennial, it is better grown as a biennial. One of the most graceful plants in this group, its large, multi-stamened flowers are held above the tufts of light green foliage. The single-flowered forms are more striking than the double forms.

9. Perennials

Hardy perennials have the great advantage that you may leave them in their pots for several years without disturbance, and they will continue to come up each year or, if they are evergreen, look good all year round. They need not be brought in during winter in mild areas, but in regions with colder winters some protection from frost may be advisable, as much for the sake of the container, if it be terracotta or stone, as for the sake of the roots of the plant. Some, such as *Agapanthus* 'Headbourne Hybrids', are hardy enough if planted in the ground, but need some protection from frost at their roots. You can either wrap straw or a material such as sacking, around the container, or take it into a shed or a cold area of the house. Whenever you leave plants in a container for more than one season, do not forget to feed them to keep them growing healthily once the nutrients in the original compost are depleted.

Propagation

Propagation of most perennials is easy. When the plant has grown into a large clump it may be divided in spring into two or more smaller plants, and each piece replaced. Some plants do not make clumps and you can propagate these by cuttings, as described for fuchsias etc. (page 28), or by seed, but these two methods usually take longer to produce a good plant.

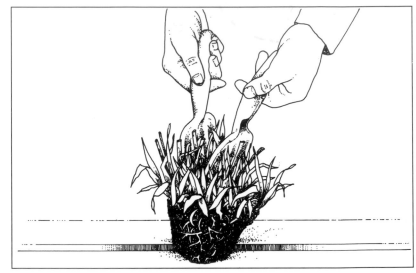

Division is best done in spring when the plants are repotted, or in autumn, after the plants have flowered.

The list given here contains only a small selection of the hundreds of perennials which will grow in containers. They are divided into two groups; those with evergreen leaves which have useful foliage throughout the year, and those whose leaves die down in winter, and which are grown mainly for their beautiful flowers.

Some tender perennials

Some tender herbaceous plants will do well outside in summer, but need to be brought indoors in winter, either into a frost-free porch or onto a window-sill. Cymbidiums, a genus of orchids, are typical of this group. They do well outside all the year in warmer climates such as the Canary Islands, but in cold countries they need to be brought in around October before the first frost, and kept rather dry in an airy but cool place; they flower in early spring and then begin growing a new fan of leaves and pseudobulb, the swollen base of the stem. They should then be watered and kept in a sunny place before being put outside again in a warm sheltered position in May, and fed and watered as are other plants.

Campanula isophylla is a pretty trailing plant which is tender and can be treated in the same way. It will flower freely in late summer and, in London at least, can be left outside all winter. There are two forms, one with pale blue, the other with white starry flowers. Agaves also need to be brought under cover in most areas, as they will rot if subjected to both wet and frost. The striped forms are very striking and give an exotic air to any planting.

Over-winter tender cymbidiums indoors.

Agave americana var. *marginata* (*right*), a striking succulent for a hot place in full sun. It is tender in cold or wet areas, where it should be brought under cover and kept dry in winter.

A large pot of *Agapanthus* 'Headbourne Hybrid' (*below*). Agapanthus are among the best perennials for tubs and large pots. Evergreen species need protection in winter, but the 'Headbourne Hybrids' are hardy enough to be left outside.

Positions for perennials

Hardy perennials vary greatly in their tolerance of different positions. For very hot places in full sun the Californian *Zauschneria californica*, a relative of the fuchsia, is a possibility. It flowers in August. Agapanthus also flower best in a very sunny place. You can plant them in a large tub where the blue heads of flowers will look good surrounded by the silver leaves of *Centaurea gymnocarpa*, or with *Alchemilla mollis*. A slightly more foreign look can be produced by the Greek spurges, *Euphorbia rigida* and *E. myrsinites* which have trailing stems of fleshy leaves and yellow flowers in spring. They will tolerate summer drought, as will the different species of *Yucca*, which will add to the exotic effect.

Most of the common herbaceous plants will tolerate partial shade, and indeed will do better in cooler places because they are less likely to dry out in hot weather. Many of the hardy *Geranium* species, such as *G. macrorrhizum* or *G.* 'Buxton's Variety' are good plants for spreading around other perennials such as day lilies (*Hemerocallis*), or true lilies or even the striking evergreen *Helleborus corsicus*, the Corsican hellebore.

In full shade where little else will grow, ferns and hostas will be your best chance of an attractive permanent planting. When you combine these with the silver leaves of *Lamium* 'Beacon Silver', and the bright lime-green feathery leaves of golden feverfew (*Chrysanthemum parthenium aureum*) and a gladdon (*Iris foetidissima*) or hart's tongue fern to give a straight line, you have made an attractive and long-lasting group which will thrive in minimal light.

Evergreen perennials

Name	Flower colour	Height and spread	Site; flowering time	Leaf shape and colour	Comments
Agave americana	Yellow, but not likely to flower	Leaves 1–3 ft (30–90 cm)	Sun; summer	Spiny grey-green (or pale-yellow striped) leaves.	*Agave* is tender in all but the warmest places; it is stiff and spiny.
Chrysanthemum parthenium aureum	White	6 in (15 cm) in leaf; 16 in (40 cm) in flower	Shade or half sun; July to August	Lime green leaves, deeply divided and ferny.	A hardy, short-lived perennial, but seeds freely. The golden form, which is the most beautiful, comes true from seed.
Euphorbia rigida and *Euphorbia myrsinites*	Greenish-yellow	8–16 in (20–40 cm) trailing	Sun; April	Bluish-green, fleshy leaves, often with orange flush.	Very useful and long-lived in poor soil and very tolerant of drought and neglect.
Hedera helix (Ivy)	(Green) usually not flowering	3 in (7.5 cm) trailing	Shade; October	Lobed or sometimes frilled leaves, variously marbled or variegated, often purplish.	Most useful as an evergreen and permanent trailer in a window box, and as a foil for colourful plants.
Helleborus orientalis (Lenten Rose)	Whitish to pink and purple	1 ft × 1 ft (30 cm × 30 cm)	Shade or half sun; February	Bold, deeply lobed, shining green leaves.	*H. orientalis* is valuable for its early flowering, *H. corsicus* for its impressive leaves.
Helleborus corsicus (Corsican Hellebore)	Green	2 ft × 1 ft (60 cm × 30 cm)	March		
Iris foetidissima (Gladdon or Stinking Iris)	Purple or cream	12–16 in × 2½ ft (30–40 cm × 75 cm)	Shade; June–July	Dark green strap-shaped leaves.	Good for its tough, healthy-looking leaves which will tolerate dry shade. Beautiful orange seeds in mid-winter.
Lamium maculatum 'Beacon Silver'	Deep pink	4 in (10 cm) trailing	Shade; April	Rounded silver leaves.	Ordinary *L. maculatum* has a silver blotch on each leaf. In 'Beacon Silver' the whole leaf is silver, and the plant is smaller.
Phormium tenax hybrids 'Sundowner' 'Yellow Queen' 'Dazzler'	Purplish	2–6 ft × 2 ft (60–180 cm × 60 cm)	Sun or half sun; summer	Upright, flat leaves in various shades of grey, red or yellow.	Hardy in all but the coldest areas. The original *P. tenax* is greyish-green and can be huge in good damp soil. The newer, named hybrids are smaller and more striking, but less hardy.
Polystichum setiferum and varieties	None	1–3 ft (30–90cm)	Shade	Variously divided fern fronds.	These two ferns have contrasting leaf shape; *Polystichum* varieties are among the most delicately and finely divided of all ferns.
Asplenium scolopendrium (Hart's Tongue)		8 in–1 ft (20–30cm)	Shade	Strap-shaped fronds.	
Vinca major 'Elegantissima'	Blue	8 in (20 cm) with trailing stems	Shade; all summer	Variegated, rounded.	Similar in general habit to ivy, but less tough and has good blue flowers. *Vinca minor* is smaller; the ordinary *V. major* is much larger.
Yucca filamentosa	White	Leaves 18 in (45 cm)	Sun; summer	Stiff grey-green (or cream striped) leaves.	Suitable plants for the centre of a large container. *Y. filamentosa* is the smallest of the *Yucca* species, often flowers and is hardy.

Helleborus orientalis

Hemerocallis

Hosta

Deciduous perennials

Adiantum pedatum (Maidenhair Fern)	None, a fern	1 ft × 8 in (30 cm × 20 cm)	Shade	Very delicate pale green fronds with scallop-shaped leaflets.	Beautiful and easy to grow in cool shade, with shelter from draughts. This species is hardy.
Agapanthus 'Headbourne Hybrids'	Blue	3 ft × 2 ft (90 cm × 60 cm)	Sun; August to September	Strap-shaped leaves in a tight clump.	Long-lasting flowers in umbels on top of bare stems. There are rare white forms. The deciduous species and hybrids are hardy, the evergreen tender except in very mild areas.
Alchemilla mollis (Lady's Mantle)	Greenish yellow	1 ft × 1 ft 8 in (30 cm × 50 cm)	Sun or half shade; June	Soft, hairy, lobed leaves.	Flowers minute in delicate groups. Leaves beautiful when fresh, and should be cut in mid-summer, when new ones will grow.
Dicentra formosa	Pink to white	1 ft × 1 ft 8 in (30 cm × 50 cm)	Shade; April	Greyish, deeply cut, delicate leaves.	Very graceful in both leaf and flower. 'Adrian Bloom' is a strong-coloured form.
Geranium wallichianum 'Buxton's Variety' (Cranesbill)	Blue	1 ft × 3 ft (30 cm × 90 cm)	Shade or half sun; June to September	Deeply cut leaves.	Very good for its long flowering season. Other geraniums are less long in flower, but are hardy, unlike pelargoniums.
Hemerocallis, various cultivars (Day Lily)	Yellow, orange, pink or red	2–3 ft × 1 ft 8 in (60–90 cm × 50 cm)	Sun or half sun; July to September	Strap-shaped leaves, fresh-green especially in spring.	Needs rich, damp soil to do well in a container.
Hosta	Mauve or white	6–20 in × 8–20 in (15–50 cm × 20–50 cm)	Shade; July	Bold, heart-shaped leaves, often striped with white or yellow.	Comes in a great variety of sizes and colours. Needs good deep soil.
Primula (Primroses and Polyanthus)	Yellow, red, pink or blue	8 in × 8 in (20 cm × 20 cm) March to May	Half sun or shade; spring–summer	Soft, rounded leaves.	Often treated as a biennial and planted in autumn to flower in spring and then thrown away.
Sedum 'Autumn Joy'	Pink	1 ft × 3 ft (30 cm × 90 cm)	Sun or half sun; September	Fleshy, bluish green leaves; good through the summer.	Flat heads of small, starry flowers which attract butterflies. Needs good soil.
Zauschneria californica	Scarlet	1 ft × 1 ft (30 cm × 30 cm)	Sun; September	Narrow, lavender-like greyish leaves.	Good in dry soil in full sun, and valuable for flowering late.

10. Bedding Shrubs and Perennials

The plants in this group are mostly tender, shrubby plants which must be kept indoors away from frost in winter, but will grow and flower well outdoors in summer. Fuchsias and pelargoniums (often referred to as 'geraniums') are both in this group. They are probably the most popular container plants throughout Europe.

Others mentioned here are perennials, but are best re-grown from cuttings every year, or every other year. Carnations, pinks, violas and pansies belong to this group. Some pansies will flower in mild weather throughout the winter. Mixed colours are best grown regularly afresh from seed, though all are capable of being perennial. Most of the named varieties must be grown from cuttings to come true.

Take a nodal cutting immediately below the node and remove the lower leaves.

Propagation

Most fuchsias can be grown easily from cuttings. These are pieces of the unflowered side-shoots, about 3 in (7.5 cm) long, which are taken from the plants in July or August. Make a clean cut just below a 'node' (which is the joint on the stem), remove the lower leaves, and insert the cuttings into a pot of cuttings-compost, which can be bought ready-mixed in bags. Having filled the pot with moist compost, insert the cuttings round the edges into holes made with a dibber or pencil. Firm the compost round them, water well, and either place the pot in a propagating case, or in a plastic bag, fastening the top over bent wires to make a 'tent' over the cuttings, and place it in a warm spot. When the cuttings are well-rooted, pot them into individual pots and keep them in a frost-free place such as a window and grow them into plants for the summer.

Geraniums, helichrysums and many other plants may also be propagated by cuttings as described, using either pieces of the older wood (hard-wood cuttings) in late summer, or the young growth (soft-wood cuttings) in the spring. Again, unflowered side-shoots are the best, and in the case of hard-wood cuttings they may be removed from the plant with a downward tug, which leaves a piece of the old wood, known as the heel, attached. Trim this up, remove the lower leaves, and insert in a cuttings-compost and treat as for fuchsias, but without the 'tent'.

The new F1 geraniums can be raised from seed to flower in their first season, but in order to do this the seed must be sown in early March and given plenty of warmth and moisture. Using this method saves the problem of keeping the plants through the winter.

If no greenhouse or frame is available, it is quite fun to try and root your cuttings in a jar of water on a warm indoor window-sill; this would be especially useful for those living in flats. Use shoots as described above, taking care to remove the lower leaves which might rot under water.

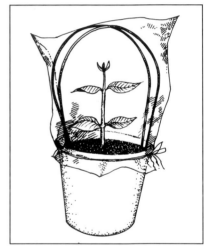

A propagating tent is easy to construct with a plastic bag and wires.

Overwintering

In areas where there is much frost in winter, old plants of most of these perennials must be taken indoors from about November to April. Most of them can be overwintered on window-sills in full light, kept rather dry and cool; they may be cut back hard if they are too large. The hardier ones will survive under an overhanging wall, again where they are rather dry. Either the old plants can be replanted outside in summer, or cuttings can be taken of the new shoots made as the weather warms up. Those which have to be raised as cuttings in summer will, of course, be overwintered indoors as young plants.

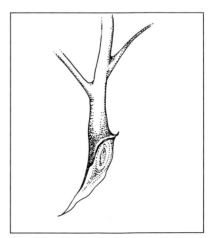

The "heel" of a hardwood cutting.

Choosing plants

Geraniums and fuchsias are rightly the most popular of this group as they will flower throughout the summer and are available in many different shades. Geraniums are the brightest and need full sun; in contrast, fuchsias have more delicacy of colour, and will do well in partial shade. Heliotrope is also very suitable for larger containers, with flat heads of rich purple flowers produced over a long period; it is sometimes called "Cherry Pie" because of its smell.

For the smaller pot or low window box try *Felicia*, the "Blue Marguerite", with beautiful pale blue, daisy-like flowers, or the spectacular gazanias with their huge daisies in the brightest oranges and other shades, contrasting with circles of black.

Pinks are lovely because of their sweet scent. Many of the modern varieties flower on and off throughout the summer; 'Doris' is a good salmon-pink, 'Houndspool Ruby' rich red-purple, 'Haytor' a pure white, with large, scented flowers.

A container needs some foil for the bright colours of fuchsias, geraniums, lilies or petunias, if it is to look handsome, and it is here that the silver-leafed bedding plants are most useful.

Upright, branching growth to hide the naked lower stems of lilies can be produced by artemisias, especially the variety 'Powis Castle', which is hardy in well-drained soil and produces huge cascades of silver on the terraces of that beautiful National Trust garden in Wales. *Senecio cineraria* is similar in habit, but has bolder leaves and heads of small, yellow flowers.

The two African helichrysums, *H. petiolatum* and *H.* 'Microphyllum', make spreading and creeping, soft grey growth, and are good for hiding the edges of the container (see page 57 and also the photograph on page 9).

Completely hanging, silver growth is made by two rather rarer creepers; *Convolvulus mauritanicus* and *Lotus berthelotii* which has strange beak-like flowers.

Fuchsia 'Claire de Lunc'

Purple heliotrope dominates this reconstituted stone urn.

Name	Flower or leaf colour	Habit and uses	Flowering time	Propagation and hardiness
Abutilon 'Ashford Red'	Salmon-red flowers.	2–4 ft (60–120 cm), upright.	May to October.	Take cuttings late summer. Tender.
Artemisia 'Powis Castle'	Silver, dissected, scented leaves.	A spreading rounded bush; a good foil for tall plants.	Insignificant.	Very easy from cuttings in summer; hardy.
Convolvulus mauritanicus	Blue-lilac flowers. Greyish leaves.	Creeping or hanging; best in sunny position.	May to September.	Cuttings with heel in June to August. Tender.
Felicia (Blue Marguerite)	Pale blue flowers. Shining green leaves.	Low, bushy up to 12 in (30 cm) high.	June to October.	Cuttings of non-flowering shoots in June to August; tender.
Fuchsia (tender varieties)	Orange, red, pink and purple to white flowers.	Growth upright or hanging; needs much water and feeding; best in half shade.	June to October.	Cuttings of young shoots in May to July; tender.
Gazania hybrids	Daisy shape flowers of yellow or orange or pastel shades with dark centres.	Creeping and mat-forming; best in full sun.	July to September.	Cuttings in July or August, or seed in spring; tender.
Helichrysum petiolatum and *H.* 'Microphyllum'	Grey leaves; insignificant flowers, but very sweet smelling.	Creeping and hanging in sun or shade; flowers only in hot years. A good foil for bright colours.	July to August.	Cuttings in June to August. Survives in very warm winters outdoors.
Heliotropium × hybridum (Heliotrope or Cherry Pie)	Purple or dark violet to pale mauve flowers.	Upright, with flat heads of sweet-smelling flowers. May be grown as a standard.	July to October.	Cuttings in September or of young shoots in February; also seed in spring. Tender.
Lantana camara	Orange, red, pink or white flowers.	Upright branching shrub. Flowers attract butterflies. Sun or half-shade.	June to October.	Cuttings in August; tender.
Lotus berthelotii	Red and black flowers. Leaves silver.	Creeping, trailing or hanging.	May and June.	Tender. Take cuttings in July or August and overwinter young plants indoors.
Mimulus glutinosus	Brownish-orange to buff or yellowish flowers.	Low, shrubby and spreading; sticky aromatic leaves; good for dry sites.	June to October.	Cuttings with heel from April to July. Hardy only in warm areas, especially near the sea.
Pelargonium cultivars	Red, purple, pink or white flowers; usually with scented leaves.	Spreading or bushy; sub-shrubby when old. Best in full sun.	June to October.	Cuttings of young wood, in August for large plants, in March for smaller plants. Tender.
Dianthus cultivars (Pinks and carnations)	Red, purple, pink or white flowers, often scented.	Mat-forming, with greyish, grassy leaves. Best in half shade.	June, then intermittent.	Hardy perennial, but best replanted every other year. Cuttings of side shoots in July.
Plumbago capensis	Pale blue flowers.	Upright. Can be grown as a standard or kept low and bushy. Best in sun.	July to September.	Tender. Cuttings with a heel in July.
Prostanthera ovalifolia	Pale mauve flowers. Scented leaves.	Upright, bushy growth. Best in full sun.	June.	Tender except in the mildest areas. Prune after flowering. Take cuttings in July.
Salvia rutilans	Red flowers.	Upright growing, shrubby when old. Scented leaves.	July to September.	Cuttings of young shoots in March, or of riper wood in September. Half-hardy.
S. patens	Pure blue flowers.	Upright, shrubby when old.	July to September.	Often grown as annual; seed in March.

Senecio cineraria	Yellow flowers. Silver, deeply divided leaves.	Robust upright growth. Often grown as an annual.	July to September.	Hardy in warm areas. Cuttings in summer or seed in spring.
Viola cultivars and pansies	Various.	Spreading and mat-forming. Can survive winter and flower very early. Winter-flowerers best in sun, summer-flowerers in half-shade.	Mainly April to June.	Hardy. Seed in late summer or spring; cuttings for early flowering in July.

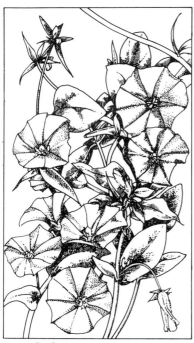

Convolvulus mauritanicus

Gazania

Lantana camara

Mimulus glutinosus

Plumbago capensis

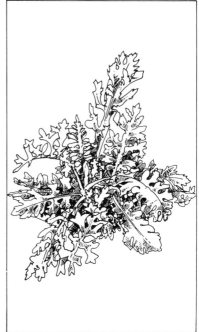

Senecio cineraria

11. Alpines

Alpine plants will grow very well in pots or window boxes. After all, in nature they are used to having to live in small pockets of soil in windy and exposed places. Attractive miniature gardens are often made in old stone sinks; they are greatly sought after by alpine enthusiasts and now so hard to find that they have almost become heirlooms.

Glazed sinks can also be used, but don't look so attractive; the plants don't mind, but if you mind you can cover the glazed outside with a cement and peat mixture which looks like stone.

How to fake an old stone sink

1. Prepare an old glazed kitchen sink by cleaning it and then painting it with an adhesive such as Evo-stik all over the outside, over the lip and about 4 in (10 cm) down the inside, and around the edge underneath. If the glaze is very shiny, it may help to scour it first with a sander on an electric drill.

2. Mix 1½ parts by volume cement, 1 part sand and 2 parts moistened moss peat (the coarse brown stuff, not the fine black) which has been sieved to remove any lumps. Add water carefully until the mixture is sticky, but will not ooze or drip.

3. When the adhesive you put over the sink is tacky, press, by hand, the cement mixture all over it, to a depth of about half an inch (1.2 cm). It will look more realistic if it is rather on the smooth side – a lumpy effect will look more informal, but more fake.

4. Allow the cement to dry well under cover, away from frost, but expose it to rain for a few weeks before planting to weather the surface a bit.

5. When planting be careful to make sure that the soil surface hides the edge of the cemented area.

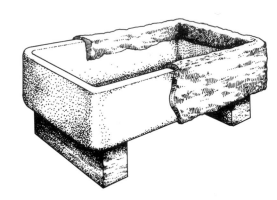

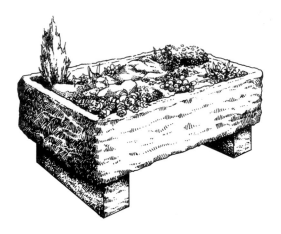

Choosing plants and preparing a sink

Sinks are especially good for growing a few tiny special plants, particularly those which grow naturally in crevices in rock. You can give them the special soil they need, with a deep cool place for the roots, and good drainage. Cushion plants such as the Kabschia saxifrages are ideal, so are delicate suckering plants such as *Campanula cochlearifolia*, the smaller gentians and dwarf shrubs such as *Salix boydii* or

Aethionema 'Warley Rose'   This is a lovely hybrid of a group of sub-shrubs which come from the Mediterranean region. The small, pink flowers are grouped in clusters on thin stems about 6 in (15 cm) high. It is very easy to grow in well drained, slightly limy soil in a sunny position, where it will spread into a neat, low, branching bush.

Campanula cochlearifolia produces hundreds of pretty, small, thimble-shaped flowers in summer and early autumn, in colours ranging through dark and pale blues to, in one form, white. The plants are easy to grow from seed and will soon spread all over an alpine trough through underground runners, so they may need to be controlled.

Potentilla nitida. Other suitable alpines are given in the table over the page. Beware of coarser plants which are tiny when you buy them, but soon smother your choice gems with lush growth. All except the smallest bulbs should be avoided because their leaves, as they wither, can damage other plants. Only the smallest crocuses, scillas or wild daffodils are fine-leafed enough to be allowed a place among the alpines.

All sinks should be provided with ample drainage material such as old broken pots, bricks or coarse gravel over the bottom, on which is placed a layer of coarse leaf-mould or peat. The soil in which the plants are to live can be made up to suit the plants which are to be grown. Most will do well in a John Innes No. 2 compost to which extra peat and sand or fine grit are added, about 2 parts compost to 1 part peat and 2 parts coarse sand or grit; for most plants crushed limestone, such as is sold for chicken or pigeon feed, is excellent. For peat-loving plants and those which hate lime, use a compost of peat and sand (which must be lime-free, not from the sea-shore) and add some sandy soil or John Innes seed compost at a rate of 2 parts peat, 1 sand or grit (non-limy), 1 John Innes seed compost, or else buy a special compost for heathers. In general the deeper the trough or sink used, the sandier the compost should be.

To make a miniature garden, much of the surface of the soil should be raised above the edge of the sink, and only just enough space left for watering.

Most alpines will need less water than other plants in the same size container, though most peat-lovers prefer a permanently damp soil.

To enhance the alpine effect, a rock or two should be placed on the surface so it appears to emerge from below ground. It also helps to provide a cool root area for the alpines, as does a surface dressing of coarse grit or gravel. In a trough for peat-loving plants, blocks of peat (such as those which are cut from a bog for burning) can be used instead of rocks. Tufa rock is especially good for alpines, and the choicest plants can be put in holes drilled into the tufa as well as around it.

One advantage of using containers for special plants is that the container, with its plants, can be moved to suit the requirements of the plant grown. For instance, *Gentiana sino-ornata* requires ample water and semi-shade in summer, but full sun and less water in autumn to open the flowers. Bulbs and Mediterranean plants may be put in a conspicuous place while they are flowering in early spring, but put either out of sight or away from any irrigation for their summer drought.

Common alpines suitable for sinks or troughs

Name	Colour of flowers	Habit	Flower-ing season	Sun/shade	Soil type	Comments
Aethionema 'Warley Rose'	Bright pink	Bushy	Spring	Sun	Limy	A beautiful small bush, with greyish leaves.
Androsace sarmentosa	Pink	Tufted	Late spring	Half sun or shade	Any	Small primrose-like flowers in umbels.
Antennaria dioica 'Rosea'	Pink	Tufted	Spring	Sun or half sun	Sandy or peaty	Small everlasting-type flowers.
Arenaria balearica	White	Creeping mat	Spring and intermittent	Half sun or shade	Any	Minute creeping mat with tiny white flowers. Good to cover shady side of sink.
Armeria caespitosa	Pink	Tight mat	Spring	Sun	Any	The neatest and smallest of the thrifts.
Campanula cochlearifolia	Blue or white	Trailing spreader	Summer	Sun or shade	Any	Easy dwarf.
Cassiope	White	Upright moss-like growths	Late spring	Half sun or shade	Peaty, no lime	Bell-like flowers on short stalks. Prefers cool site.
Dianthus alpinus	Pink	Tight mat	Late spring	Sun	Limy	Large-flowered dwarf pink.
Draba aizoides	Yellow	Tufted	Early spring	Sun	Limy	Easy and drought tolerant. Will grow on walls.
Dryas octopetala	White	Creeping on surface	Late spring	Sun	Limy	Flowers followed by fluffy seed heads. Plant near edge.
Erinus alpinus	Purple or pink	Tufted	Early summer	Sun or half sun	Limy	Seeds itself; will grow on old walls.
Gentiana acaulis	Deep blue	Tufted	Late spring	Half sun	Any	Often shy-flowering but wonderful when it does well.
Gentiana sino-ornata	Bright blue	Creeping annual stems	Autumn	Light shade in summer – sun in autumn	Peaty – no lime	Easy to grow, but best in the north.
Gentiana verna	Deep blue	Tufted	Spring	Sun or half shade	Lime with peat	Small, but intense deep greeny-blue, starry flowers.
Gypsophila repens 'Rosea'	Pink	Creeping	Spring	Sun	Any	Plant to sprawl over the edge.
Hebe buchananii 'Minor'	White	Rounded bush	Spring	Sun or half sun	Peaty or sandy	Cypress-like growth.
Helichrysum coralloides	White but seldom flowers	Upright growths		Half sun	Peaty or sandy	Coral-like green and white woolly stems.
Juniperus communis 'Compressa'	Bluish-green leaves	Columnar bush		Sun	Any	One of the slowest dwarf conifers.
Leontopodium alpinum (Edelweiss)	White	Tufted	Summer	Sun	Limy	Longest-lived when starved.

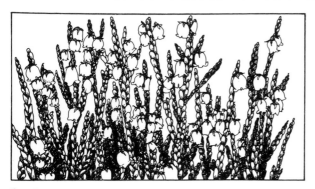

Cassiope

Leontopodium alpinum

Linaria alpina	Purple and orange	Tufted	Summer	Sun	Limy	Tiny, bright, snapdragon-like flowers.
Linum arboreum	Yellow	Bushy	Spring	Sun	Lime	Requires warmth.
Lychnis alpina	Pink	Tufted	Summer	Sun	Sandy	
Morisia monanthos	Yellow	Tufted	Early spring	Sun	Sandy	Jagged dandelion-like leaves. Bright flowers on the ground.
Origanum amanum	Pink	Tufted, annual stems	Summer	Sun	Limy	Beautiful tubular flowers and aromatic leaves.
Penstemon rupicola	Magenta	Creeping	Early summer	Sun	Any	Plant to spread over edge.
Picea mariana 'Nana'	Grey-green leaves	Rounded bush		Sun	Any	Dwarf conifer.
Potentilla nitida	Pink	Low, creeping	Summer	Sun	Lime	Beautiful strawberry-like flowers on a silver low bush.
Primula auricula and hybrids	Yellow and various	Tufted	Spring	Half sun or shade	Limy	Flowers also vary from blue in *P. marginata* to red in *P. hirsuta* and all colours between.
Primula farinosa	Pink	Tufted	Spring	Half sun or shade	Lime with peat	Bird's Eye Primrose.
Rhododendron dwarf types	Various	Low, bushy	Spring	Half sun or shade	Peaty, no lime	All the dwarf types are suitable for containers and prefer cool sites.
Salix boydii	Silky, grey catkins	Craggy bush	Spring	Half sun	Peaty	Interesting round leaves.
Saxifraga 'Jenkinsae'	Pale pink or white	Tight mat	Early spring	Half sun	Sandy	The dwarfest and earliest saxifrage.
Saxifraga longifolia	White	Tufted	Early summer	Half sun	Lime	A single large, silvery rosette. If possible plant vertically.
Saxifraga cochlearis 'Minor'	White	Tight mat	Summer	Sun	Lime	A mat of silvery rosettes.
Sempervivum arachnoideum	Deep pink	Tight mat	Summer	Sun	Lime	A small houseleek with cobweb-like hair on the leaves.
Veronica rupestris	Blue	Creeping stems	Late spring	Sun or half sun	Lime	Plant to spread over edge.

12. Wall Plants

Actinidia kolomikta

Carpenteria californica

Most walls and fences can be considerably enhanced by the addition of climbing plants, and, when space is at a premium, these vertical areas are valuable extensions to the garden.

There are two kinds of plants which can be grown on, or against, such structures. Firstly, there are the true climbers which attach themselves to the wall by clinging with their tendrils (e.g. sweet peas), by twining around the support (e.g. honeysuckle), or by putting out clinging aerial roots (e.g. ivy). The second category comprises many shrubby plants which will grow happily up against a wall but these need artificial support and tying in (e.g. *Ceanothus*). In addition, there are many annual plants which will scramble up a trellis, providing a quick and colourful covering (e.g. nasturtiums, runner beans).

Details are given below.

Abutilon megapotamicum Yellow and red flowers from May to October. Small shrub. Half-hardy, so only suitable for mild areas. Needs a warm wall.

Actinidia kolomikta Grown for its leaves, which have striking pinky-white markings. An elegant, vigorous, plant. It prefers a south- or west-facing wall.

Campsis radicans Trumpet-shaped, orange and red flowers in August and September. A tall climbing shrub which supports itself with aerial roots.

Carpenteria californica White, scented flowers in June and July. Requires full sun; only reliably hardy in mild areas. Protect from cold winds.

Ceanothus 'Autumnal Blue' Soft blue flowers from July to October. Vigorous and hardy. Evergreen.

C. thyrsiflorus Blue-mauve flowers in May and June. Free-flowering. Hardy. Evergreen.

Clematis There are many species and hybrids suitable for growing in containers; those listed are generally easy to grow and all are available commercially. Clematis like to have their heads in the sun and roots in the shade, so it is a good idea to shade the surface of the soil in the container and to prevent it drying out by putting a layer of pebbles (or gravel) around the base of the plant. For the same reason, you should use the largest container you can. A small selection of some of the best species and hybrids is given here.

Clematis species

C. armandii Creamy-white, fragrant flowers in April. Evergreen. Mild areas only.

C.a. 'Apple Blossom' Pinkish-white flowers also in April. As above.

C. montana White flowers in May and June. Very vigorous.

C.m. 'Elizabeth' is pink and scented.

C.m. 'Rubens' is rose-pink.

C.m. 'Tetra-rose' is rosy-mauve.

C. orientalis Yellow flowers from August to October. Attractive, silvery seed-heads produced in autumn.

Clematis hybrids

'Barbara Jackman' Purple flowers with plum stripe in May and June. Fairly vigorous.

'Bee's Jubilee' Pink with carmine stripe from May to July. Same colouring as 'Nelly Moser', but more intense.

'Comtesse de Bouchaud' Pinky-mauve flowers from June to August. Will do well on a north-facing wall.

'Ernest Markham' Rose-red from June to September. Very free-flowering.

'Hagley Hybrid' Light pink flowers from June to September. Vigorous and free-flowering.

'Lady Northcliffe' Lavender flowers from June to October. Fairly vigorous.

'Lasurstern' Deep lavender blooms from May to September. Fairly vigorous.

'Mrs Cholmondely' Light lavender-blue flowers May to July. Free-flowering.

'Nelly Moser' White blooms tinted pink from May to September. Best on a north wall, as colour bleaches in sun.

'Perle d'Azur' Sky-blue flowers July to August. Free-flowering.

'Ville de Lyon' Carmine-red flowers July to September. Vigorous.

Cobaea scandens Purple, bell-shaped flowers from May to October. Sow seeds under glass in March; plant out in early June. Needs south- or west-facing wall. Will flower until the first frost.

C.s. 'Alba' Creamy-white form of the above.

Eccremocarpus scaber Orange, tubular flowers June to October. Fast growing perennial which climbs by leaf tendrils. Fully hardy in warm areas only. May be raised annually from seed.

Fremontia californica (Syn. **Fremontodendron californicum**) Golden-yellow flowers May to October. Only suitable in mild areas. Full sun, and south- or west-facing wall preferred.

Ceanothus thyrsiflorus

Clematis 'Ville de Lyon'

Ipomoea purpurea

Passiflora caerulea

Hedera (Ivy) There are many different ivies which are suitable for growing in containers, all of which are evergreen, and attach themselves to the wall by means of aerial roots. The following are some of the more spectacular:

H. canariensis 'Gloire de Marengo' Large leaves, deep green in the centre, edged silvery white.

H. colchica 'Paddy's Pride' Large leaves, with yellow centre, merging into pale green, and edged dark green.

H. helix 'Buttercup' Pale golden.

H.h. 'Goldheart' Small dark green leaves with bright yellow centres.

H.h. 'Glacier' Small, silvery-grey leaves edged with white.

Honeysuckle (see **Lonicera**)

Ipomoea (Morning Glory)

I. purpurea Purple flowers July to September. Half-hardy annual. Prefers sheltered, sunny position.

I. tricolor 'Heavenly Blue' Blue flowers, which last only one day, borne from July to September. Annual; needs full sun. Soak the seeds in water for 24 hours before sowing.

Ivy (see **Hedera**)

Jasminum nudiflorum (Winter jasmine) Yellow flowers from November to February. Valuable winter-flowering shrub.

J. officinale White, fragrant flowers June to September. A twining climber, which may grow to as much as 30 ft (9 m). Requires sheltered position; good for shade.

Kerria japonica 'Pleniflora' Double yellow flowers in spring. Vigorous shrub, which will grow happily against a wall.

Lathyrus odoratus (Sweet Pea) Scented, pink, white, mauve, red or purple flowers from June to September. Annual. Sow seeds under glass in March. Plant out in early May. Feed copiously, and pick off *all* faded flowers.

Lonicera (Honeysuckle) There are many different climbing forms, most of which will grow happily in containers; only a selection is listed here.

L. × americana Scented, white flowers turning yellow, tinged purple, on outside, in June and July. Very vigorous and free-flowering.

L. caprifolium Creamy-white, scented flowers in June and July. Fairly vigorous.

L. 'Dropmore Scarlet' Scarlet, tubular flowers July to October.

L. japonica 'Halliana' Heavily scented,

white flowers becoming yellow June to October.

L. periclymenum Creamy-white flowers, yellow on outside of petals June to September. Vigorous. (This is the common honeysuckle or woodbine).

L. × tellmanniana Long, tubular, orange-yellow flowers in June and July. Prefers shade, or semi-shade.

Morning Glory (see **Ipomoea**).

Nasturtium (see **Tropaeolum majus**).

Passiflora caerulea (Passion flower) Bluish-white flowers in summer and autumn. Requires warm, sunny wall.

Pyracantha coccinea 'Lalandii' Masses of orange-red berries in autumn. Clusters of small white flowers in early summer. Strong-growing, stiff shrub.

Roses There are so many different types of climbing and rambling roses available that the only way to choose is to look at the catalogue published by a good rose nursery; some of the most popular of these roses are:

'Albertine' Salmon-pink, scented flowers in summer. Vigorous, but prone to mildew.

'Caroline Testout' Scented, double, rose-pink flowers in summer.

'Elegance' Slightly scented, pale yellow flowers in early summer, and sometimes again in the autumn. Vigorous.

'Gloire de Dijon' Scented, apricot-pink flowers early and throughout season.

'Mme. Grégoire Staechelin' Scented, coral flowers early summer. Vigorous, but prone to mildew.

'Parkdirektor Riggers' Crimson and recurrent.

'Pink Perpétue' Rose-pink and recurrent. Moderately vigorous, so suitable for restricted space.

'Zephirine Drouhin' Scented, pink and recurrent. Moderately vigorous, but prone to mildew.

Solanum crispum 'Glasnevin' Deep purple-blue flowers from July to September. Requires full sun and south or west wall.

Sweet Pea (see **Lathyrus**)

Teucrium fruticans Pale blue flowers from June to August. Silver foliage. Evergreen. Requires plenty of sun.

Tropaeolum majus (Nasturtium) Shades of orange, red and yellow from June to September. Easily grown from seed. Prefers poor soil.

Vitis vinifera 'Brandt' (Vine) Leaves turn yellow and orange in autumn. Will produce small black grapes in suitably warm conditions.

Solanum crispum 'Glasnevin'

Vitis vinifera 'Brandt'

13. Shrubs and Trees

Shrubs and trees provide the most permanent form of planting in containers. Some are grown for their height. Others are used primarily for their foliage, to make a green background for more exotic and colourful annuals or, if they are evergreen, to give some greenery in winter. A few are grown mainly for their flowers, but the majority of shrubs and trees provide leaves for most of the year as well as a display of flowers for a season.

Trees tend to be grown primarily for their shapes and their height. Not many are suitable for container growing without special treatment and extra care. The art of Bonsai, the oriental custom of dwarfing trees (but training them into natural-looking shapes) calls for continuous dedication and skill on the part of the grower; the tree relies on a small amount of root in a shallow container, and must be watered even more often than daily in dry weather. Even in large containers such as half barrels, a tree will need a lot of care and water if it is to remain healthy, requiring to be fed while it is growing in spring.

Architectural shrubs

These useful plants are called 'architectural' because of their strong, striking shapes and bold leaves with deep lobes or even spines. The mahonias such as *M. japonica* and 'Charity', and *Fatsia japonica* are two common examples of this type of shrub. They are good at all seasons of the year, and will form the basis of a group of plants, even in shady corners. A very different shape can be found in the palm-like *Cordyline indivisa*; and you can grow real palms such as the dwarf *Chamaerops humilis* in mild areas or if you bring them under cover in winter.

Tender shrubs

Those who live in large cities have one big advantage over country dwellers; shrubs or plants of doubtful hardiness will often thrive in a large city because the danger of frost is lessened, and summer temperatures are even hotter. This can provide a marvellous opportunity to grow rather tender plants, perhaps some seen normally in the Mediterranean, such as oleanders, pomegranates and myrtles. Camellias also do very well in cities, especially London, as they like warmth and tolerate shade. They also do well in tubs. Few are better than the pink hybrid 'Donation' which will make a fine bush up to six feet high (1.8 m), covered in early spring with huge flowers.

Soils for shrubs

Most shrubs will do well in ordinary soil such as John Innes compost no. 3. For long-term plantings, com-

Mahonia japonica

Fatsia japonica

posts with loam are better than the loam-less peat-based composts. Some shrubs require a lime-free compost or at least one which is acidic. Camellias, rhododendrons and azaleas are the most familiar shrubs which need acid soil, and hydrangeas need it too if you want them to be a good blue colour. For these the soil should be mainly peat or forest bark, with lime-free sand and some loam, as is described in the section on soils on pages 10–11.

Propagation of shrubs

As you are not likely to need many plants of any one shrub, their propagation can be left to nurserymen, who produce them by the thousand. Nevertheless most can be reproduced by taking cuttings in July of new but hardening shoots; pot these in a mixture of peat and coarse sand, and keep them shady and moist, enclosing their pot in a polythene bag (see page 28). Alternatively, mature hardened shoots can be taken in autumn and left to root slowly during winter and spring. Generally it is better to propagate evergreens from summer cuttings, and deciduous shrubs from autumn cuttings, but summer cuttings of deciduous shrubs will often root well, and should be grown on as much as possible so that they survive the winter.

Chamaerops humilis

Azaleas provide a brilliant display in early summer, but can only be grown in an acid compost.

Name of Plant	Approx. height and habit	Colour of flowers/foliage	Flowering time	Other points
Acer palmatum (Japanese Maple)	Up to 15 ft (4.5 m), usually spreading.	Striking foliage in shades of red, gold and orange.	Foliage colours in autumn.	Prefers moist, well-drained soil.
Azalea – evergreen varieties like 'Hinomayo', the most free-flowering.	3–4 ft (90–120 cm)	Pink, red, purple and white flowers.	Early summer.	Needs acid soil.
Bottle-brush (*Callistemon linearis* or *rigidus*)	Up to 6 ft (1.8 m), graceful.	Brush-like spikes of scarlet flowers.	July	Requires well-drained soil and a sunny position.
Box (*Buxus sempervirens*)	Up to 10 ft (3 m), bushy.	Dark, glossy green leaves. (Variegated forms also available.) Inconspicuous flowers.	Evergreen	Can be clipped into formal shapes.
Camellia 'Adolphe Audusson' (red), 'Donation' (pink)	Up to 8 ft (2.4 m), bushy.	Dark green, shiny leaves and red, pink or white flowers.	Flowers in early spring.	Requires lime-free compost. Suitable for north aspect. Camellia roots must never be frozen.
Chamaerops humilis (Dwarf Fan Palm)	Trunk usually up to 3 ft (90 cm), but taller in old specimens.	Small, yellowish, insignificant.	Evergreen	Full sun with good drainage.
Citrus (oranges and lemons)	Up to 4 ft (1.2 m), upright.	Dark green, glossy leaves. Clusters of white fragrant flowers.	April–June	All citrus are tender.
Conifers				There are many different dwarf species and hybrids, most of which will grow happily in tubs. They are valuable for their attractive evergreen foliage and often striking shape.
Chamaecyparis 'Minima Aurea'	Up to 2 ft (60 cm), erect.	Gold foliage.		
C. pisifera 'Boulevard'	Up to 4 ft (1.2 m), pyramidal.	Silvery blue foliage.		
Juniperus media 'Old Gold'	Up to 3 ft (90 cm), spreading.	Golden foliage.		
J. virginiana 'Grey Owl'	Up to 2 ft (60 cm), spreading	Grey foliage.		
Convolvulus cneorum	2–3 ft (60–90 cm), bushy.	White flowers, silvery leaves.	May–September	This bushy, evergreen shrub prefers a sunny position.
Cordyline (Cabbage Palm), *C. indivisa*	3–4 ft (90–120 cm) palm-like.	Handsome green leaves with red or yellow mid-ribs.		These plants are only half-hardy and are best brought indoors in the winter.
Eucalyptus gunnii (Gum Tree)	Up to 6 ft (1.8 m), upright.	Leaves blue-green or grey. White flowers.	July–August	Prefers full sun, well-drained soil, and protection from draughts.
Euonymus fortunei 'Emerald Gaiety'	Compact, up to 2 ft (60 cm).	Silvery-green variegated leaves.		Small evergreen shrub.
E.f. 'Emerald and Gold'	Dwarf, up to 1½ ft (45 cm).	Golden-variegated leaves.		Evergreen shrub.
E.f. 'Silver Queen'	Up to 6 ft (1.8 m), compact.	Green foliage with bright silvery margin.		Evergreen, compact shrub which can grow tall against a wall.
E. japonicus 'Microphyllus'	Up to 3 ft (90 cm), dense, compact.	Small, dark green leaves.		Evergreen shrub.
Fatsia japonica	Up to 8 ft (2.4 m), erect.	Handsome glossy, evergreen fig-like leaves. White ivy-like flowers.	October	Best in a sheltered position; fatsias thrive in city gardens.

Hebe 'Autumn Glory'	Compact habit, 2–3 ft (60–90 cm).	Deep violet-blue flowers.	July–September	A large family of dwarf shrubs with evergreen leaves and bottle-brush type flowers of pink, blue, mauve and white. Hebes prefer a sunny sheltered position.
H. glaucophylla 'Variegata'	Compact habit, 2–3 ft (60–90 cm).	Greyish-green foliage; small white flowers.	July–August	
H. 'Great Orme'	Up to 4 ft (1.2 m), upright, bushy habit.	Bright pink flower spikes.	May–July	
Hydrangea macrophylla – a) Hortensia	3–4 ft (90–120 cm), bushy.	Pink, white and blue flowers.	July–September	Blue hydrangeas will only keep their colour in acid soils – in other soils blueing powder must be applied.
b) Lacecap – 'Blue Wave',	3–4 ft (90–120 cm), tall, bushy.	Blue/pink.	August–September	Best in semi-shade.
'Lanarth White'	Compact growing.	White with blue or pink centres.		Also for semi-shade.
Lavandula (Lavender) –				All types of lavender prefer well-drained soil in full sun.
L. spica 'Hidcote'	1–2 ft (30–60 cm).	Violet flower spikes.	July–September	
L.s. 'Munstead'	Compact, 2–3 ft (60–90 cm).	Dark blue.	July–September	
L.s. 'Twickel Purple'	2–3 ft (60–90 cm), compact.	Lavender blue-purple.	July–September	
L. stoechas	2 ft (60 cm), loose.	Dark purple.	May–July	Very aromatic.
Mahonia japonica, *M. × media* 'Charity'	Up to 6 ft (1.8 m).	Yellow, very sweet-scented. Evergreen.	November–January	These grow best in partial shade, with the roots kept cool.
Myrtus communis (Common Myrtle)	2–3 ft (60–90 cm), bushy.	Fragrant white flowers.	July–August	Evergreen. Requires sheltered position against south or west wall.
Nerium oleander (Oleander)	Up to 6 ft (1.8 m), bushy.	White, yellow, apricot or pink.	June–October	Evergreen shrub. Tender. Poisonous.
Potentilla fruticosa 'Elizabeth'	3 ft (90 cm), bushy.	Primrose flowers.	June–September	Sometimes sold under the incorrect name *P. arbuscula*.
Punica granatum (Pomegranate)	5–7 ft (1.5–2.1 m), bushy.	Red flowers.	June–September	Suitable for cultivation outdoors only in the mildest areas.
Rhododendron 'Blue Diamond'	3 ft (90 cm), compact.	Lavender-blue.	April–May	Lime-free, peaty compost required. Vast numbers of species and hybrids are commercially available; dwarf forms are obviously the most suitable for tubs.
R. 'Elizabeth'	2–3 ft (60–90 cm), spreading.	Rich red.	April–May	
R. yakushimanum	2 ft (60 cm), compact.	Pink fading to white.	May–June	
Roses – many different types:				All roses need constant feeding.
Floribunda – e.g. 'Iceberg'	5 ft (1.5 m), branching.	White.	June–July Sept–October	Hardy deciduous shrubs.
Hybrid Tea – e.g. 'Colour Wonder'	3 ft (90 cm), dwarf.	Salmon-orange. Slight scent.	June–October	Sun or partial shade. Well-drained fertile soil.
Miniature – e.g. 'Baby Gold Star'	14 in (35 cm), dwarf.	Yellow semi-double flowers.	June–July	Ideal for window boxes and wall pots.
Old shrub – e.g. 'Fantin Latour'	5 ft (1.5 m), bushy.	Pink, double flowers.	June–July	Heavily scented; flowering season shorter than modern shrub roses.
Taxus baccata 'Fastigiata' (Irish Yew)	Up to 6 ft (1.8 m), densely bushy.	Evergreen. The golden-leaved form 'Aurea' is also pleasing.		Clipped yew looks good in containers in a formal setting.

14. Bulbs

Of all flowers bulbs will give the brightest display with the least effort and skill on the part of the gardener. In most of them the flowers are already formed inside the bulb when they are bought, and need only water and suitable temperature to come to perfection. Some will even flower without water, while the bulb is still almost dormant! Because the gardener is buying a ready-made flower, it is especially important to buy good quality bulbs.

An early spring show of crocus and *Iris reticulata*

Two categories

Bulbs fall into two categories according to their time of growing. The most familiar outdoor ones such as daffodils and tulips, start growing in the autumn, and make their roots in the winter, ready to flower in spring. These are completely hardy, and indeed need a cold winter to develop properly. Some bulbs however start growing in spring and flower in the summer. They are mostly not hardy as they come from tropical regions, and they need to be stored out of the frost in winter. More examples of the two sorts are given over the page. A few flower in autumn and grow through the winter making their leaves in spring. Examples of these, such as cyclamen and colchicum, are also given. Most bulbs go dormant soon after they have flowered. The few weeks between flowering and dormancy are critical to the bulb's future health. They should be watered and fed during this period, and then left to become rather dry as the leaves fade. They may then be stored dry until planting time comes round again. Alternatively they may be thrown away after flowering, or planted into the open garden, and new bulbs may be bought each year.

Buying good bulbs

Most bulbs in the shops originate in Holland where the big wholesalers have been established since the seventeenth century. Only a few, such as daffodils, are mostly grown in England. Because of this many bulbs are beginning to dry up by the time they reach the shops, so it is important to choose carefully those which are firm and plump, and avoid those that are either soft or hard and dry. Hyacinths especially are delicate, and those which have been bruised are more likely to rot before flowering. Dwarf irises such as *Iris reticulata* are susceptible to a disease aptly called ink spot. It shows as black patches and streaks on the pale coat of the bulb, and any which are badly affected should be avoided. Snowdrops are better moved while growing, and are likely to come poorly from dried and imported bulbs. Many specialist bulb nurseries sell them in spring while growing, and they are easy to establish when bought in this way. Lilies are best planted in autumn, although they are summer flowering, and so they should be planted as early as possible after they appear in the shops. If they do seem dry and shrivelled when bought, they should be planted in moist peat for a week or two to recover before being planted.

Planting

Planting depths and times are important and differ from species to species; they are given in the tables overleaf. Suitable soil for most bulbs is one which is well drained with a good mixture of sand, humus and loam such as is found in the John Innes compost. The fibre sold for bulbs is only suitable for those which are grown in bowls indoors. Most of the small bulbs are better for having a handful of coarse sand put round each bulb or group when planting. Spring-flowering bulbs need to be planted in early autumn, but tulips will flower satisfactorily if planted rather later than other bulbs, i.e. not until November. It is very important that bulbs should not become dry between planting and flowering: premature drying out is one of the commonest causes of failure. Bulbs should only be dry after they have flowered when the leaves begin to go yellow. It is also important that the leaves are not cut off while they are still green, even if they do look untidy, because they contain and manufacture the substances required for the next year's flowering. Only when they have died down may they be cut off.

The photograph opposite shows different bulbs in flower. The display is bright but brief. A longer succession of flowers can be had by planting larger later-flowering bulbs towards the bottom of the container, such as lily-flowered tulips, followed by earlier-flowering, smaller species tulips towards the surface. Continuous interest could therefore be had in one container or window box from February to May. The tables overleaf give details of flowering times in the London area, so the relative flowering times of each bulb can be seen and a selection made to give a succession in any area. This can be achieved at virtually any time of the year.

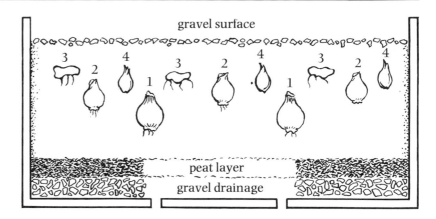

Cross-section of a container to show planting for succession. The rows should be staggered.

1. Late tulip, single (or double – better in a windy site, as it is shorter).
2. Early tulip – *T. kaufmanniana*
3. *Anemone coronaria*
4. *Iris reticulata* or *I. danfordiae*

Plant Associations

Because most bulbs have rather uninteresting leaves, a better show can be made if they are planted with other more leafy plants. Ivy, especially the forms with dark leaves, forms a good foil for pale early bulbs, and prevents the flowers being splashed with mud by heavy rain. Anemone leaves, especially those of *A. coronaria*, are attractive and delicate, similar to parsley. Small early bulbs can also be planted in the same pot as hostas or *Agapanthus*. They will have made their growth before the large plants grow up. There are many different creeping plants suitable for growing beneath lilies to shade the surface of the soil and hide their bare stems. *Helichrysum petiolatum* with its delicate grey leaves and spreading habit is especially suitable, and petunias, lobelias or ivy-leaved geraniums have a similar effect. The bold leaves of cannas are set off by the more ferny foliage of *Artemisia* 'Powis Castle', which although hardy will grow quickly from cuttings to make a good bedding plant. In the photograph this artemisia is planted with a purple petunia around *Lilium lankongense* hybrid. As a general rule plants will associate well if their leaf shapes or habit make a pleasing contrast, and their roots are active at different levels in the soil. Always remember that a thickly planted container in full growth will need much more water and feeding than one newly planted, or containing only one tree or shrub.

The table below gives the most important characteristics of a selection of bulbs that are easily obtainable through bulb suppliers and garden centres. They have been arranged according to their season of flowering, so that it is easy to plan a succession of flowers throughout the year.

Spring-flowering

Plant in the autumn, if possible in September.

Recommended selection	Colour	Height	Month of flowering	Number required	Depth to plant	Planting site, etc.
Galanthus nivalis (Snowdrop)	White	4 in (10 cm)	1–2	12	2 in (5 cm)	Moist soil or shade.
Leucojum vernum (Snowflake)	White and green	8 in (20 cm)	2	8	3 in (7.5 cm)	,,
Iris danfordiae	Yellow	4 in (10 cm)	2	12	5 in (12.5 cm)	Sun or shade.
Iris histrioides	Blue	5 in (12.5 cm)	2	8	3 in (7.5 cm)	Sun or half shade. Sandy soil.
Iris reticulata and all cultivars	Purple	6 in (15 cm)	2	12	3 in (7.5 cm)	Sun; sandy soil.
Eranthis hyemalis (Winter Aconite)	Yellow	3 in (7.5 cm)	2	10	3 in (7.5 cm)	Shade or half shade.
Crocus chrysanthus – all cultivars	Yellow to blue, striped	4 in (10 cm)	2	12	3 in (7.5 cm)	Sun or half shade.
Crocus tomasinianus	Purple	4 in (10 cm)	2	12	3 in (7.5 cm)	Sun or shade.
Crocus 'Large Yellow'	Yellow	5 in (12.5 cm)	3	6	4 in (10 cm)	Sun.
Bedding Hyacinths	White, pink, yellow or blue	6 in (15 cm)	3	5	4 in (10 cm)	Sun or shade.
Muscari armeniacum (Grape Hyacinth)	Mid-blue	5 in (12.5 cm)	4	12	4 in (10 cm)	Sun.
Narcissus 'February Gold'	Yellow	8 in (20 cm)	2–3	6	4 in (10 cm)	Sun or half shade.
Narcissus 'Ice Follies'	Cream	16 in (40 cm)	4	4	4 in (10 cm)	Large and blousey.
Narcissus 'Mount Hood'	White	16 in (40 cm)	4	4	4 in (10 cm)	A white daffodil.
Narcissus 'Carlton'	Yellow	18 in (45 cm)	4	4	4 in (10 cm)	
Tulipa kaufmanniana and cultivars	Cream to red striped	8 in (20 cm)	3	10	3 in (7.5 cm)	Sun. Stony good soil
Tulipa turkestanica	White, starry	6 in (15 cm)	3–4	10	3 in (7.5 cm)	,,
Tulipa praestans 'Fusilier'	Intense red	9 in (23 cm)	3–4	6	4 in (10 cm)	,,
Tulipa fosteriana and cultivars	Red or white	9 in (23 cm)	4	4	4 in (10 cm)	,,
'Early' Tulips single or double	Various	12–14 in (30–35 cm)	4	4	4 in (10 cm)	Sun or half shade.
'Darwin' Tulips	Various	24 in (60 cm)	4–5	4	5 in (12.5 cm)	,,

Name	Colour	Height			Depth	Notes
'Lily-flowered' Tulips	Various	20–25 in (50–63 cm)	4–5	4	5 in (12.5 cm)	,,
Fritillaria imperialis (Crown Imperial)	Red or yellow	18 in (45 cm)	4	1 or 4	6 in (15 cm)	Sun. Stony good soil.
Fritillaria persica 'Adiyaman'	Black	24 in (60 cm)	4	1 or 4	6 in (15 cm)	,,
Fritillaria meleagris (Snake's Head Fritillary)	Purple or white	9 in (23 cm)	4	6	4 in (10 cm)	Moist peaty soil.
Trillium grandiflorum	White	6 in (15 cm)	4	5	3 in (7.5 cm)	Shade, half shade, with leafy soil.
Trillium sessile	Purple.	8 in (20 cm)	4	3	3 in (7.5 cm)	,,
Erythronium 'Pagoda'	Yellow	10 in (25 cm)	4	5	4 in (10 cm)	,,
Erythronium 'White Beauty'	White	8 in (20 cm)	4	5	4 in (10 cm)	,,
Erythronium dens-canis (Dog's Tooth Violet)	Pink, marbled leaves	4 in (10 cm)	3	10	4 in (10 cm)	,,
Cyclamen repandum	Pink, marbled leaves	3 in (7.5 cm)	4	5	2 in (5 cm)	Sun or half shade.
Cyclamen coum	Deep pink	2 in (5 cm)	2–4	5	2 in (5 cm)	Shade or half shade.
Arum italicum	Leaves veined with white	10 in (25 cm)		3	4 in (10 cm)	,,
Ipheion uniflorum	White to pale mauve	6 in (15 cm)	3–4	8	3 in (7.5 cm)	Sun or half shade.
Anemone blanda	Blue, pink or white	4 in (10 cm)	3–4	10	3 in (7.5 cm)	Sun or half shade.
Anemone fulgens	Brilliant red	6 in (15 cm)	3	8	3 in (7.5 cm)	Sun.
Anemone coronaria – St Brigid Anemone (double), De Caen Anemone (single)	Red, pink or blue	6 in (15 cm)	3–5	8	3 in (7.5 cm)	Sun. Will flower in winter if forced.
Anemone nemorosa (Wood Anemone)	White to pale blue	4 in (10 cm)	3–4	10	3 in (7.5 cm)	Shade or half shade, in leafy moist soil.
Camassia esculenta (Quamash)	Purple-blue	10 in (25 cm)	6	10	3 in (7.5 cm)	Sun, but moist peaty soil.

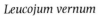

Leucojum vernum

Fritillaria meleagris

Erythronium 'White Beauty'

Tigridia pavonia, a bulb (corm) from Mexico, is not reliably hardy except in mild areas. Planting it at a depth of 4 in (10 cm) in the pot, protecting it in winter and keeping the pot in a warm, dry spot in the garden will help it survive cold winters. Its gorgeous flowers are produced in a variety of colours, including shades of red, gold and white, and are often exquisitely spotted. Each large bloom lasts for a day only, but as the bulbs produce several spikes of flowers, the display is prolonged.

Summer-flowering

Plant if possible in the autumn.

Recommended selection	Colour	Height	Month of flowering	Number required	Depth to plant	Planting site, etc.
Allium karataviense	Silvery flowers	4 in (10 cm)	5	3	4 in (10 cm)	Sun and stony soil.
Allium moly	Yellow	6 in (15 cm)	6	8	4 in (10 cm)	Sun or half shade, moist soil.
Allium christophii	Purple, starry	10 in (25 cm)	7	5	4 in (10 cm)	Sun.
Gladiolus byzantinus	Red-purple	20 in (50 cm)	5	8	5 in (12 cm)	Sun.
Lilium candidum (Madonna Lily)	White	36 in (90 cm)	6	3	1 in (2.5 cm)	Sun. Rich limy soil. Deep pot, but planted shallow.
Lilium regale	White, purple outside	36 in (90 cm)	7	3	6 in (15 cm)	Sun or half shade.
Lilium Asiatic hybrids esp. 'Enchantment'	Orange to red	36 in (90 cm)	7	3	6 in (15 cm)	Sun or half shade.
Lilium Trumpet hybrids	White to pink or yellow	40 in (1 m)	7	3	6 in (15 cm)	Sun or half shade.
Lilium martagon album	White	36 in (90 cm)	7	3	6 in (15 cm)	Shade or half shade.
Lilium auratum (Golden Rayed Lily of Japan)	White and yellow, red spots	40 in (1 m)	7–8	3	6 in (15 cm)	Sun or half shade. Sandy, peaty, rich soil.
Lilium speciosum	Pink	40 in (1 m)	8–9	3	6 in (15 cm)	Sun or half shade.

Summer-flowering

Plant in the spring. Protect from frost in winter.

Pleione limprichtii – hardy orchid	Pink	4 in (10 cm)	4	10	0	Plant on surface. Peaty soil in shade.
Gladiolus nanus hybrids	Pink or white	15 in (38 cm)	6	5	6 in (15 cm)	Plant in winter and protect from frost, sun.
Gladiolus callianthus (Acidanthera)	White, fragrant	25 in (63 cm)	8	10	6 in (15 cm)	Sun. Moist peaty soil.
Tigridia pavonia (Tiger Flower)	Red, gold, white	12 in (30 cm)	6	10	4 in (10 cm)	Sun.
Zantedeschia aethiopica (Arum Lily)	White	30 in (75 cm)	7	1	6 in (15 cm)	Sun, very rich soil, plenty of water.
Gloriosa superba	Red and gold	30 in (75 cm)	8	6	6 in (15 cm)	Warm, sheltered spot, rich soil.
Eucomis bicolor	Green	20 in (50 cm)	8–9	3	6 in (15 cm)	Sun, rich soil.
Canna 'Lucifer'	Red and yellow	20 in (50 cm)	8	3	6 in (15 cm)	Sun, rich soil. Start in warmth indoors.
Sprekelia formosissima	Dark red	12 in (30 cm)	8	5	4 in (10 cm)	Warm sheltered spot.
Begonia 'Giant Double'	Various	12 in (30 cm)	7–8	3	2 in (5 cm)	Half-shade. Moist rich soil.
Begonia 'Pendula'	Various	15 in (38 cm)	7–8	5	2 in (5 cm)	Suitable for hanging baskets.
Tropaeolum tuberosum	Orange	to 60 in (1.5 m)	9–10	5	4 in (10 cm)	Climbing on a trellis. Sun or half shade.

Autumn-flowering

Plant in August and keep outside all winter, dry in summer.

Nerine bowdenii	Pink	18 in (45 cm)	9–10	5	1 in (2.5 cm)	Sun. Plant bulbs on surface of deep pot.
Sternbergia lutea	Yellow	6 in (15 cm)	9–10	8	3 in (7.5 cm)	Sun.
Colchicum speciosum	Pinkish or white	9 in (23 cm)	9	3	6 in (15 cm)	Sun, moist soil in spring. Leaves large.
Cyclamen hederifolium (Wild Cyclamen)	Pink	3 in (7.5 cm)	8–10	3	1 in (2.5 cm)	Sun or half shade. Leafy soil with stones.

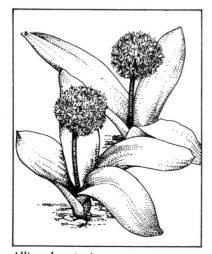

Allium karataviense

Pleione limprichtii

Cyclamen hederifolium

15. Herbs

Many herbs grow happily in containers, and in addition to being useful for cooking, also look attractive. Bay, rosemary and sage need good-sized containers and a sunny position. All three are evergreen, and this helps to clothe the bare containers in winter. Bay can be clipped into interesting shapes, and will eventually make a large shrub. Other smaller herbs which are suitable for window boxes are chervil, chives, parsley, and thyme. Basil is also well worth growing for its delicious flavour, but in this country has to be treated as an annual.

Many annual and biennial herbs can be raised easily from seed, or bought as young plants. Clump-forming perennials like chives are propagated by division – the plant is lifted and broken into smaller clumps (see page 24). Shrubs like bay and sage are propagated by cuttings (see page 28).

Cultivation

Herbs in containers need good drainage, and most also require plenty of sun. It is important to provide large enough containers for the shrubby herbs, although the more compact types will often thrive in small pots or window boxes. Special herb pots with soil pockets are available, but in my experience these are not always successful, as the lower plants tend to miss the rain and water from above. If you want to grow herbs in one of these containers you must ensure that each 'pocket' is carefully fed and watered. When planting herbs fill the base of the container with pebbles or broken pieces of pot, cover this with peat (or leaf mould if you have it) and then fill up to within an inch (2.5 cm) of the rim with good compost (e.g. John Innes). Raise the containers a little off the ground to ensure that water does not collect at the base of the pot.

Basil (*Ocimum basilicum*) Grown in Britain as an annual, making a low, bushy plant. Sow seed under glass in April, or buy young plants in early summer. Delicious with tomato salad in particular; pinching out the tips for culinary use will encourage its bushy habit.

Bay (*Laurus nobilis*) Fairly hardy in warm areas; grows happily in a container (although obviously not to the same height as it would in the open ground). Propagation is by cuttings taken during late summer; dipping the ends in hormone powder will encourage rooting. Insert the cuttings in a sandy soil in a cold frame. Bay leaves are used in soups and stews, and can be dried satisfactorily.

Borage (*Borago officinalis*) An easily grown annual, making a large bristly hairy plant in good moist soil. Sow seed in spring. The blue flowers are very beautiful.

Caraway (*Carum carvi*) A biennial or perennial carrot-like herb, grown for its aromatic seeds. Sow in late spring, and harvest them in late summer before they fall.

Chervil (*Anthriscus cerefolium*) A dainty annual, like a small hedge-parsley. Seed may be sown in autumn, for winter use, or in spring. The young leaves are used, and have a delicate aniseed-like taste.

Chives (*Allium schoenoprasum*) Chives are easy to grow in most soils, and like plenty of water. The bulbs increase rapidly, and the plants can be divided every few years in the autumn. Chopped leaves add flavour to salads, omelettes, potatoes, and many other savoury dishes.

Dill (*Anethum graveolens*) An annual with leaves rather like fennel, and yellow flowers. The seeds are used to make gripe-water. The leaves are good in salads and are commonly used for pickling gherkins.

Garlic (*Allium sativum*) Garlic is easy to grow in

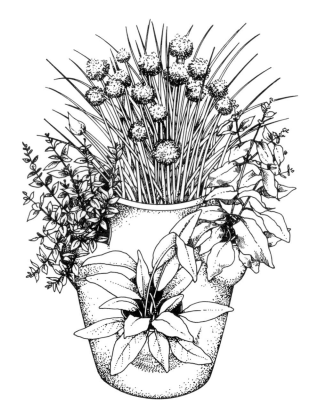

A herb pot showing holes in the side for different herbs. These pots may also be used for growing strawberries (see page 53). It is often difficult to grow plants satisfactorily in the side holes, especially the lower ones, as they get insufficient water and light. Plant the most vigorous herbs such as sage in the lowest holes and the upright ones like chives or basil in the top.

Borage

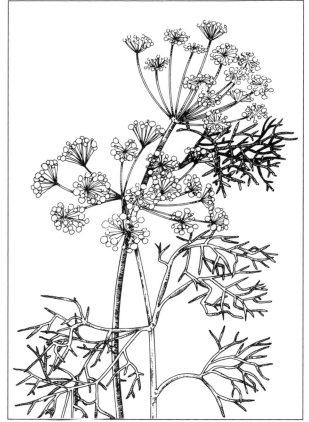

Dill

good sandy soil in a sunny place. Individual cloves may be planted in autumn in warm areas or in early spring, and harvested and dried in late summer.

Horseradish (*Armoracea rusticana*) This perennial needs really deep rich soil to make good sized roots. It will grow in shade and make tufts of lush dark green leaves and sometimes branching stems of small white flowers.

Lemon Balm (*Melissa officinalis*) A herbaceous perennial, very easy to grow but of limited use. The leaves smell of lemon and can be used to make a delicate tea.

Pot Marjoram (*Origanum onites*) A dwarf shrub which requires well-drained soil, and a warm, sheltered position. Propagate by seed or cuttings. Used in meat dishes.

Mint (*Mentha spicata*) This herb needs a moist, rich soil in semi-shade; try never to let the soil dry out completely. Delicious with peas and new potatoes and for making a mint sauce.

Parsley (*Petroselinum crispum*) Parsley seed germinates somewhat erratically, so it is often best to buy young plants in the spring. Strictly speaking this is a biennial plant and so will have to be replaced every other year. Used as a garnish, also in soups, salads and sauces.

Rosemary (*Rosmarinus officinalis*) An evergreen shrub which requires a sunny, sheltered spot, preferably against a south-facing wall. Imparts flavour to most meat (particularly lamb) and casseroles. The liquid obtained from boiling leaves in water makes a

useful tonic for dark hair.

Rue (*Ruta graveolens*) The most widely available rue in commerce is *R.g.* 'Jackman's Variety'. It is a hardy evergreen shrub, with greyish, strong-smelling leaves, and rather insignificant yellow flowers. Propagate by cuttings. Add sparingly to salads.

Sage (*Salvia officinalis*) A small shrub with greyish leaves; propagation is by cuttings taken in spring. This herb likes full sun, and a sheltered position. Used in stuffings for poultry.

Savory (Winter savory – *Satureja montana*; Summer Savory – *Satureja hortensis*) Both species of savory have narrow leaves and purplish or whitish flowers. Summer savory is an annual, winter savory a perennial, shrubby at the base. Both grow best in a sunny position; they are strong tasting and should be used sparingly.

Sorrel (*Rumex acetosa*) Sorrel is grown for its acidic spinach-like leaves, so needs a rich peaty soil with plenty of water, and a position in semi-shade. It is perennial and seeds sown in spring should make good plants by the end of the summer.

French Tarragon (*Artemisia dracunculus*) French tarragon is to be preferred to the hardier Russian, if it is to be used for cooking. It is a perennial with underground creeping runners and floppy stems with narrow leaves. It needs a sunny site, but good soil and plenty of water while growing.

Thyme (*Thymus vulgaris*) A compact, evergreen shrub; likes full sun and well-drained soil. Can be grown successfully in a 'parsley pot'.

16. Fruit

Many types of fruit can be grown in containers, but for practical purposes only very few are really successful. A few suggestions follow, but with a large enough container, a mild climate, and plenty of enthusiasm, you may have success with others not mentioned here.

Use a pot just large enough to take the feeding roots (thinner branching roots) when spread out horizontally. Do not be tempted to use a larger pot than is necessary to start with, but give the tree a larger pot each time it is repotted, until it reaches its final size.

If the tree is grafted, as most fruit trees are, be sure to keep the graft above soil level. When buying apples, be sure that they have been grafted onto an 'M9' or 'M26' dwarfing rootstock. With pears the equivalent is called 'Malling quince C'. These dwarfing rootstocks produce trees of suitable vigour, which fruit sooner.

Be sure to use a soil-based compost such as John Innes no. 3, not a peat or soil-less compost. If kept under cover, water sparingly in winter, but water more in early spring as the buds begin to swell, and continue watering until the fruit is ripe. Feeding is important; give sulphate of ammonia if more growth is needed, otherwise a general high potassium and phosphate fertilizer such as Tomorite to encourage good fruiting.

Pear trees are especially suitable for growing in pots. Nowadays most fruits are easy and cheap to buy in good condition, but pears are among the more difficult to store and buy at the right moment. Furthermore they are easy and satisfying to train.

In an espalier the central stem is continued upwards until the desired height is reached. Laterals are encouraged at regular intervals and trained as horizontally as possible. Fruiting spurs, which are short stubby side shoots, form in the second or third years.

To encourage the production of the fruiting spurs, cut back side shoots in summer to about 6 in (15 cm) or four leaves from the main horizontal branch. Only the terminal shoot of each branch should be allowed to grow, until its desired length is reached.

If the pear or other tree is not to be trained against a wall, it is better to train it into a pyramid. Spur shoots must still be encouraged, but the side branches are shorter and more numerous.

With many fruits it is necessary to grow two different varieties together so that they may cross-pollinate each other. A nurseryman will know which varieties are cross-compatible; in pears two good ones to begin with are 'William Bon Chrétien' and 'Doyenne du Comice' or 'Conference' as they will usually be in flower together and will pollinate one another. With **apples** also some varieties are more suitable for growing in pots, and 'Cox's Orange Pippin' is one of the best for this purpose.

Some fruits, such as **peaches** and **nectarines**, are self-compatible, and a good set of fruit can be had when only one tree is grown. **Cherries** are mainly self-sterile, but the cultivar 'Stella' is good in pots as it is self-compatible, producing sweet black fruits.

In fruits such as peaches and nectarines, the flowers are produced not on spurs but on the previous year's shoots. For these it is therefore important not to shorten the side branches, but only the very strong leafy shoots which appear on vigorous trees.

Although they are so different in appearance, **figs** also fruit on the tips of the previous year's short shoots. Any growth not required to increase the size of the

A pear tree in a pot trained as an espalier.

tree should be pinched out in early summer after about four leaves have formed. Leading shoots can be stopped a little later. Figs do well in pots as they do not grow wildly at the expense of fruiting as they often do when planted out; in fact it is a positive advantage to restrain the roots of a fig.

After the flowers have opened, and the fruit set, care must be taken to keep the tree well watered, and not allow the pots to dry out. Established trees will benefit at this stage from a dose of liquid feed. It may also be necessary to thin the fruits, if too many have formed. Most fruit trees lose a proportion of their fruits naturally around mid-summer, but further thinning may also be needed to get the final fruit to a good size. Figs do not need thinning however, as their fruits ripen over a period of several weeks in succession, until stopped by cold weather.

After the excess fruits have fallen or been removed, and as the fruits begin to swell, the pots should be top-dressed with a good rich fertilizer such as John Innes base and dried blood mixed with some damp peat. Put about 2 in (5 cm) of this mixture on the top of the compost in the pots, if necessary raising the edge of the pot with a metal strip. Keep this layer moist, so that feeding roots grow into it. Continue watering after the fruit has been picked, to build up a good supply of flower buds for the next year. At this stage keep a look out for red spider, which can damage the leaves and weaken the trees.

Any repotting should be done in October. Young, vigorously growing trees may need moving into a larger pot; well-established ones should have the top few inches of soil replaced, or be repotted in new compost.

Grape vines will do well in pots, and look attractive even when not fruiting. Some varieties will ripen well outside in warm summers in southern England, but most need warmer conditions than they get here.

Most grapes are climbers, so will need some support, and if they grow well can be trained to form the roof of an arbour, as is often seen in Mediterranean countries. The size of the pot, and therefore the size of the root system, will determine the amount of top growth you can expect. Soil should be well drained John Innes no. 3 compost with some extra grit added; peat composts are not suitable.

Correct pruning is not difficult once the few principles are known. Vines fruit on spurs growing from main stems called 'rods'. These spurs are formed early in spring from buds near the base of the previous year's growth, so all shoots should be pruned, in winter, back to two or three buds. This one-year-old wood will be paler and redder than the grey older wood. Only where the extra length is needed for training, should new spurs be left long.

Pinching out of long shoots will also be required in summer. Fruiting spurs should be pinched out two or three leaves beyond the bunch, and any side shoots which form, pinched at one leaf. Long spurs should be pinched when they have reached the desired length, and again the side shoots kept pinched back.

Various complicated training systems will be found in books on grape growing, but the plants will make fruit and look more attractive when trained for decoration, so long as the principles of pruning are borne in mind.

Some varieties will ripen outside better than others. 'Black Hamburg' is a familiar easy variety, which will ripen in warm years against a wall. 'New York Muscat' may be more reliable in England, but no varieties will ripen sweet fruit regularly in the open, even south of London.

If they are going to ripen properly, and be used for eating, the bunches should be thinned. Only one bunch per spur should be allowed to develop, and about half the berries on each bunch should be cut out with a pair of pointed scissors, when they are the size of small peas, leaving the rest evenly spaced to swell without crowding.

Liquid feed such as Tomorite should be given regularly while the vine is in leaf if it is fruiting, or Liquinure (high nitrogen) if growth is required. For colourful leaves, starve the plants after they have made good growth.

The fruiting spurs on a grape vine are cut back to two buds after leaf-fall, as shown on the right.

Strawberries need a good humus-rich soil, and will do well in peat composts. They should be planted into pots or grow-bags in August or September, so that they are well established before winter. If young plants are bought in spring, they should not be allowed to crop heavily their first year, but grown into large plants, and all the runners should be removed as they form. Regular feeding with liquid manure will help to build up good plants, and this will be vital if a peat compost is being used.

Good strawberry plants may be grown in large pots, tubs or window boxes, but special strawberry pots or barrels with holes in their sides are often seen for sale (see page 50). If you are growing strawberries in one of these, make sure that the lower plants get enough water and light, or they will fail. A roll of wire netting, filled with gravel placed down the centre of the barrel at the time it is filled with soil, will help water penetrate the bottom of the compost and reach the lowest plants. Some of the plastic barrels designed for strawberries have built-in watering tubes or capillary matting, which ensure that all the plants are watered equally.

17. Vegetables

For city dwellers with only limited space, growing a few vegetables in containers can be fun, and the rewards of "picking your own" are bound to be appreciated.

Many of the well-known varieties *will* grow in containers, but success depends on the size of the pot, quality of compost, regularity of watering and feeding, and current weather conditions.

Growing bags

A mention should be made here of 'growing bags'; these are polythene bags filled with a peat-based compost which often includes a slow-release fertilizer. They are particularly convenient for the flat-dweller as the preparation of the soil has already been done. The fertilizer is generally active for only one year, but if you provide extra nutrients you can use them for a second year quite satisfactorily. They are highly recommended for most types of vegetables, including tomatoes, but are not suitable for root crops, such as parsnips, which need a far greater depth of soil. Growing bags can, of course, be used for flowers also, but they do not look very aesthetic, unless you place them inside another container, to cover the plastic; there are some containers available commercially specifically for this purpose.

Suitable vegetables

Whilst it is possible to grow almost any vegetable in a container (provided the latter is large enough), it is generally more rewarding to grow either the more short-lived and shallow-rooted plants such as lettuce, or dwarf French beans or, if you have a south- or west-facing wall, those plants that flourish in the sun, e.g. tomatoes, aubergines or peppers.

Tomatoes can be particularly rewarding and are relatively easy to grow; there is also the advantage that young plants can be bought and planted straight into the container, which is helpful to those with no facilities for raising plants from seed. The new, small-fruited cultivars are, in my experience, particularly successful (see the list of varieties).

If you have a fence, why not try runner beans or peas? Beans, in particular, cover the area quickly and have attractive red or white flowers as a bonus.

Potatoes can be grown in a barrel (or an especially deep container – see the illustration), but the barrel needs to be a good size, so only attempt this if you can spare the room.

In addition to the crops mentioned above there are several others worth trying, like radishes, courgettes and spring onions.

List of selected cultivars suitable for growing in containers

Aubergine
  'Long Purple'
  'Moneymaker'
  'Short Tom'

Suitable for outdoor-growing only in warm areas, ideally against a sunny, sheltered wall. Set out young plants at end of May in suitable container, e.g. growing bag. Provide plenty of water, and nip out the tops to promote bushy growth.

Bean (dwarf French)
  'Loch Ness'
  'Masterpiece'
  'Prince'
  'Tendergreen'

French beans prefer a site well sheltered from strong winds. For successful germination do not sow seed until the soil has really warmed up (i.e. about the middle of May). It can be a good idea to cover the container with a sheet of plastic for about two weeks prior to planting, to help warm the soil. Loch Ness is suitable for colder areas.

Bean (runner)
  'Achievement'
  'Désirée'
  'Prizewinner'

Do not sow seed until the end of May or early part of June (see above). Give plenty of water in dry weather. Train up a wall or trellis.

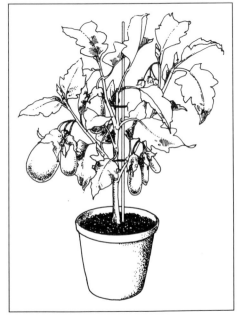

Aubergine

Capsicum (Sweet pepper)
'Ace'
'Canape'

Only suitable for mild areas; select a warm, sheltered spot, preferably against a south-facing wall. Set out young plants at the end of May, or beginning of June. Warm the soil (as with beans) or provide cloches, if you have them.

Carrot
'Rondo'

Early, stump-rooted cultivars are the best for growing in containers. Carrots prefer light, well-drained soils and a warm, sheltered site.

Courgette
'Emerald Cross'
'Zucchini' ('True French')

Courgettes like very rich, well-drained soil, so try to get hold of some compost and work this into the soil prior to planting. Seed can be sown outside at the end of May.

Courgette

Lettuce – Butterhead
'Tom Thumb'
– Cos 'Little Gem' 'Paris White'
– Crisphead 'Minetto' 'Webb's Wonderful'
– Looseleaf (non-hearting) 'Salad Bowl'

All types of lettuce like a light but fertile soil, with plenty of water during dry weather. By selecting different cultivars, and sowing a few seed at weekly or fortnightly intervals, one can have lettuce from early spring to autumn.

Potato (early)
'Foremost'
'Maris Bard'
'Pentland Javelin'

Deep, well-drained tubs or proprietary planters should be used. Cover the base of the tub with a layer of potting compost, to a depth of about 6 in (15 cm). Place 4 or 5 seed potatoes on this, cover with another 6 in (15 cm) layer of compost, and water. As the shoots appear, add more compost, leaving about an inch (2.5 cm) of foliage showing; carry on doing this until the foliage appears above the rim of the container, watering well.

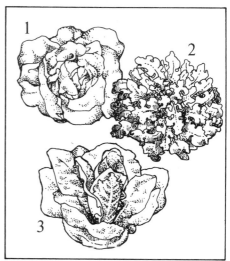

Lettuces – 1. Tom Thumb; 2. Salad Bowl; 3. Paris White.

Radish
'French Breakfast'

Ensure good drainage in the container, but water frequently while the plants are maturing. Seed can be sown at intervals from March to September. Once the plants are fully grown they should be eaten quickly, and not left in the ground for very long.

Spring onion
'White Lisbon'

Seed can be sown at intervals from March to June.

Tomato
'Gardener's Delight'
'Minibel'
'Tiny Tim'

If raising from seed, sow in spring indoors in gentle heat. Prick out into small pots, and harden off well before planting out. Alternatively, buy young plants (usually available towards the end of May) and plant out straight into the container where they are to fruit.

A potato barrel

18. Plant Associations

One of the most enjoyable aspects of planting containers is to be able to experiment, on a small scale, with different plants and to see how they look together. There are many possible permutations of form and colour, and the following ideas may help to start you off.

When planning the planting of your container take into consideration its size and shape, position and background; also consider whether you propose to site it in sunshine or shade. These factors will make a difference to your choice of plants. Try and build up in your mind a picture of how the plants will look when they are fully grown. A large urn needs a tall plant in the centre to give height and plants trailing down the sides will give a softening effect.

Spring planting

In the spring you will be able to make a choice from a large selection of bulbs and early-flowering plants, such as pansies, polyanthus and wallflowers, which, together with the early bulbs such as snowdrops, crocus, and daffodils, will give a most pleasing display of colour. For instance, daffodils in a window box would look well with *Muscari* (grape hyacinths) growing in front of them, and with a variegated ivy trailing along the front of the box. The early double tulips last in flower for several weeks and could be underplanted or edged with crocus, polyanthus, *Bellis perennis* (double daisy), pansies, or violas. The bedding hyacinths could be treated in the same way.

Dwarf bulbs, e.g. *Iris reticulata, Crocus, Chionodoxa, Anemone coronaria* are especially useful for window boxes, and look very effective mixed with a dwarf perennial such as aubretia. Wallflowers, polyanthus, and forget-me-nots form an attractive combination, and thrive in full sun, but for a shady site it would be better to omit the wallflowers.

The dwarf type of evergreen azalea often known as Japanese Azalea, is available in many shades of red, orange, pink and white and in conjunction with violas and pansies gives an early splash of colour. Camellias, such as 'Donation', 'Adolphe Audusson' or 'J. C. Williams', could be substituted for azaleas, but remember that both azaleas and camellias need a lime-free soil; in fact, in a chalky area these plants can be grown successfully only in containers. Remove the heads of pansies as they fade and you will have a succession of flowers lasting many weeks.

A large terracotta pan planted with perennials suitable for a very shady corner. Blue-green leaves of *Hosta tokudama* contrast with golden Feverfew, *Lamium* 'Beacon Silver' and purple Bugle. The sword-like leaves of Iris and Hart's Tongue fern, and the delicate beech fern complete the arrangement.

Summer planting

Geraniums (correctly called pelargoniums) are among the most useful plants for a summer display; the trailing ivy-leafed type, such as the pale pink 'Mme Crousse', red splashed with white 'Rouletta', or the desirable 'L'Elégante' with very pale mauve petals and variegated leaves, is excellent in every type of tub or hanging basket, and associates well with grey-leafed *Helichrysum*, purple heliotrope, and fuchsias, all of them lasting well into the late summer.

You will find *Helichrysum petiolatum* an invaluable creeper for containers, as the roots are very small in comparison with the ultimate spread of the plant, and it can be tucked in a pot and grown to arch over the sides or grow flat over the surface. As well as the grey-leafed type, which acts as a foil for so many colours, there is a variegated form with green and yellow foliage; and also a yellow form often sold under the name 'Limelight', and *Helichrysum* 'Microphyllum' with smaller, silvery leaves. These shrubs are not reliably hardy, so if you cannot take them inside during winter, take a few cuttings in late summer to provide plants for next year.

Purple heliotrope teams up well with fuchsias such as 'Lena' or 'Chillerton Beauty', or with pink antirrhinums, the pink candytuft (*Iberis*) 'Pink Queen', and *Ageratum*.

Fuchsias are especially suitable for hanging baskets; you could try an upright one with a trailing variety, such as 'Cascade', over the sides. In a tall pot a standard fuchsia gives height, and the sides of the pot could be covered with ivy-leafed geraniums and blue or purple trailing lobelia.

The grey-leafed *Senecio cineraria* 'White Diamond' (often known as *Cineraria maritima*) provides an excellent foil for fuchsias, and other pink or magenta plants. The tender blue *Felicia pappei* would also go well with grey foliage in a tub in a sunny position.

Convolvulus mauritanicus is a low-growing trailing plant with beautiful, brilliant blue-mauve flowers. Try it with orange *Impatiens* or the apricot *Mimulus glutinosus* – again for a warm sunny spot only.

Petunias and variegated ivy make a good combination of foliage and flower.

Try the following ideas for effective planting –

—*Abutilon* 'Ashford Red' with *Lysimachia nummularia* ("Creeping Jenny")
—African or French Marigolds with dark blue *Lobelia* 'Crystal Palace'
—*Fuchsia* 'Thalia' with *Lobelia* 'Cambridge Blue'
—Nemesias, nasturtiums and trailing lobelias
—Nemesias with dwarf bedding dahlias
—White impatiens and white petunias and alyssum
—Blue hydrangeas and blue lobelia

For permanent planting
—Dwarf *Rhododendron* 'Elizabeth' and blue periwinkle
—*Camellia* 'Donation' or Japanese azalea, 'Hinomayo' with the dwarf broom, *Cytisus* × *kewensis*
—*Artemisia* 'Powis Castle' with the garden pink, *Dianthus* 'Doris'

Winter

For permanent planting to give colour throughout the winter in your containers, the dwarf conifers look well with *Euonymus japonicus* 'Microphyllus' or the trailing *Euonymus radicans* 'Variegatus'. Variegated periwinkle is another attractive trailing plant as is *Lamium maculatum*, or variegated ivy, and these could be associated with the winter-flowering heathers. In addition to grouping different plants within one container good effects can be obtained by moving various containers to give changing plant associations. You can also group several pots containing one sort of plant together, taking into account the size and shape of your containers and perhaps raising some of them on bricks or steps to give height.

19. Pests and Diseases

Plants grown in window boxes and pots are not immune from the usual troubles which affect all garden plants, but the troubles which affect them worst tend to be different, and in general are more easily cured. There are four major groups of problem; those caused by sucking insects, those caused by chewing insects and other animals, those caused by fungal diseases and those caused by deficiencies in the soil.

Sucking insects

Many of the worst pests thrive in warm conditions and are especially bad on plants which have been kept too dry at the roots. Greenfly, blackfly and whitefly are among the commonest pests – minute, winged insects, the first two of which are commonly called aphids. They attack especially young and delicate shoots or the undersides of leaves, sucking the plant's juices, causing curling of the leaves or deformation of the petals. When adult they fly from one plant to another, soon starting a new colony.

Another group of sap-sucking pests are the scale insects, which look like small brown blisters on the stems of woody plants or on evergreen leaves. They are very common on climbers such as vines, or on the stems of ferns. The presence of scale insects on your plants, and of greenfly or blackfly is often revealed by ants running frantically up and down the stems to 'milk' the greenfly and scale insects for the sticky sweet juice they can be made to exude.

The third common sucking insect, the red spider, is the most minute and probably the most damaging. It is not a true spider, but is a mite and visible only to those with good eyesight. The young are pinkish, though the largest specimens are almost black. Hundreds of them will swarm over the underside of a leaf. Even though the insects themselves are difficult to see, the results of their presence are all too apparent. The affected leaves go spotty and finally yellow between the veins, before dying and falling off.

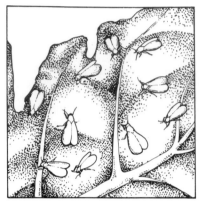
Whitefly

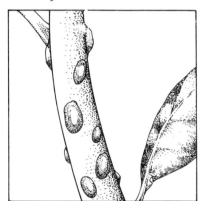
Scale insects

Control of sucking insects

Small infestations are easily controlled by using an aerosol with insecticide in it. Many of the modern ones are fast-acting, based on pyrethrum-type chemicals and designed to be harmless to humans and not persistent. If you keep a keen eye on your plants you can stop a bad attack of aphids gaining a foothold. If, however, the area to be sprayed is large, it may be better to buy a sprayer and a bottle of insecticide concentrate and use that. One well-known product is Abol-X which contains more than one insecticide and is systemic; that is, it gets into the sap of the plant and kills any sucking or leaf-eating insect. It can either be sprayed onto the plant or applied as a drench to the roots, so avoiding possible damage to bees or butterflies. It can only be used if the plants are not going to be eaten. Another similar, more modern insecticide which I have used with success is called 'Tumblebug'.

Chewing insects and other pests

The worst of the chewing insects are the vine weevils. They are difficult to see and, once they have become established, are very hard to get rid of, causing a lot of damage meanwhile. The adults are small, matt black beetles and are nocturnal, feeding on leaves and flowers and leaving characteristic rounded scallops in their edges. The grubs are more sinister, about $\frac{1}{4}$ inch ($\frac{1}{2}$ cm) long, fat, white, curled and slightly hairy. They eat the roots and the soft bark of plants just below ground level, or bore up into fleshy stems, eating out their hearts. The first sign of their presence is the collapse and imminent death of the plant. Control is not

Red spider mite

easy. Nearly all vine weevils are female, and just one can lay over a thousand eggs in one season, on a wide variety of plants. Primulas, cyclamen and lilies are specially favoured, but even such tough plants as ivies can be deprived of their roots and killed. The adult beetles can be found with a torch on warm evenings, sitting on the leaves; pick them off with great care or they will drop to the ground and lie quite still, imitating a crumb of earth. In the daytime they may sometimes be found hiding under old leaves, loose pots or other rubbish. Insecticide, such as gamma BHC, can be incorporated into the compost as a preventative against the grubs, or plants in which their presence is suspected can be repotted or watered with a soil drench, such as Abol-X, if the plants are not going to be eaten.

Other nocturnal, creeping, leaf-biting insects which may cause trouble are the earwigs, which love many-petalled flowers such as dahlias or chrysanthemums, but cause only superficial damage. Wood-lice will also often eat growing plants and roots. You can kill both these if you dust crannies and other likely hiding places with a soil insecticide, and you can discourage their attentions in future if you pick up any rubbish around in which they can hide.

Slugs and snails may sometimes be troublesome, especially in spring and autumn and in wet weather. They usually leave a tell-tale trace of slime around the part of the leaf they have been eating. They can be killed by blue slug pellets, but these should not be put where cats or dogs may find them. On warm, damp nights slugs and snails will be found feeding on the choicest succulent leaves and they can then be collected and killed by squashing or by putting them in a jar of salt. Alternatively a lettuce leaf or two will act as bait to attract them and in the morning they will be found sheltering under it.

Earthworms are also pests to plants grown in containers, as they destroy the soil structure, which leads to waterlogging. They can be kept out of pots by plugging the drainage holes with the kind of glass wool that is sold for cladding, or by standing the pots on special saucers (see page 17). If they are established in a pot they can be removed by repotting the plant, or killed with wormkiller.

Ants also do little direct damage, but are harmful because they distribute and encourage aphids or make nests in pots. They can be reduced by poisoned syrup or by ant-killers in powder form.

Birds, especially sparrows, can be a real nuisance, damaging or eating the flowers of primroses and crocuses in early spring, or eating the buds of climbers such as clematis. Black cotton stretched over susceptible plants will usually be enough to discourage them.

Vine weevil

Earwig

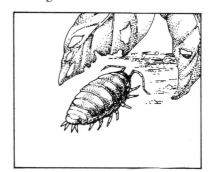
Wood-louse

Diseases and deficiencies

Fungus diseases attack all kinds of plants, but most of them are unlikely to cause trouble, and those that do can be controlled with sprays. There are two main groups of pathogenic fungi; mildews which look like white powdery deposits and affect the upper leaves of plants especially in dry weather, and moulds which are commonest on the lower parts of plants and are encouraged by damp, close conditions. The mildews are best sprayed with sulphur compounds or with dinocap, and prevented by making sure that the plants are well watered in dry weather. Grey moulds (*Botrytis* species) which cause affected parts to die can be prevented by better ventilation or by spraying and drenching with benlate. Other diseases, such as rose black spot, are troublesome only on one type of plant, and are also controllable by sprays available from all garden centres.

Deficiency diseases, in which the leaves of plants go yellow and grow slowly, though the plants are otherwise healthy, are caused either by waterlogging or by growing lime-hating plants in limy or chalky soil, or by watering them with hard tap water. If you suspect that the unhappy appearance of a plant is caused by deficiency, first examine the soil and the roots to see if the soil is compacted, too damp and poorly drained, and the roots dead or at least not growing actively. If the soil looks in bad condition, repot the plant in fresh soil.

Rhododendrons, azaleas and camellias are all likely to suffer from iron deficiency caused by too much lime in the soil. It may be treated by using sequestrene, now available in granular form, or by watering the plants with old tea and tea-leaves, which form a good mulch so long as the surface does not become compacted and prevent the even penetration of water into the compost. Other deficiency diseases are not likely to be encountered, as most liquid fertilizers have trace elements added to them already.

20. Siting Containers

The best place to put your container is where it will look most effective, and where it is most wanted; the choice of plants to fill it will then depend on what will grow best in that particular aspect.

The importance of light

In the sections dealing with different types of plants (annuals, perennials etc.) I have indicated the position in which each plant will thrive, whether in full sun, half sun, or shade. Half sun, and half shade will be a common position in town gardens where the sun may be on the plants for, at most, half the day or probably only for a few hours each day, but there is otherwise more or less full light. Plants which tolerate shade will thrive in north-facing places where there is no sun at all, or only a little in early morning and late evening; but even these need a certain amount of light and may not thrive when shaded by tall buildings. Ferns and *Impatiens* are two of the plants which will grow in places like basements that are too dark for most others.

The problem of wind

Shade is not the only problem. Some sites are unsuitable because they are too sunny and too exposed, especially to drying winds. The adverse effects of these must be counteracted with frequent watering, and by using large containers of impervious material, such as plastic. In areas where wind is a problem and especially near the sea, you will have to use wind-tolerant and low-growing, bushy plants. It is worth noting that the grey-foliaged

The massed plants in this pot benefit from being given a very sheltered position on the garden terrace.

These well-filled pots of fuchsias and geraniums stand in a warm south-facing position.

plants such as *Artemisiu* 'Powis Castle' are normally successful on the coast. Hebes, phormiums and many other shrubs from New Zealand are wind-tolerant and thrive in cooler places. Mediterranean shrubs such as rosemary or Californian ones such as *Ceanothus* are good in sunnier sites, combined with dwarf bulbs or creeping perennials such as gazanias.

Sheltering plants on balconies

Window boxes, especially above ground-floor level, roof gardens and balconies in cities are often remarkably exposed because the streets act as wind tunnels, and draughts eddy round the buildings. The provision of shelter is an important first step towards growing a wide range of plants on a balcony and persuading them to look happy, flower freely, and so produce the best effect everyone is aiming at. Primary shelter can be made by using trellis on which climbers are trained. *Clematis orientalis* is probably the most wind- and drought-tolerant of clematis, and most *Ceanothus* are also good. *Lonicera japonica* 'Halliana' will grow, but not as bushily as in sheltered gardens, and I have found its scent disappointing on a draughty balcony. It is very important to give these shelter-producers a large container, with good soil and plenty of water and feeding, so that they can support as much growth as possible.

Advantages and disadvantages of walls

Another point to remember is that window boxes and other containers, when placed near a wall, do not get as much rain as pots standing in the open, and invariably need extra and frequent watering in summer and during cold dry spells in winter. The walls, especially in cities, are a good protection against frost, and many plants, normally considered tender in the British Isles, will grow outside all the year round. In London, for example, many oleander plants stand outside all year, do not lose their leaves in winter, and flower well in summer.

Index

64

Dr Martyn Rix is the former botanist at the Royal Horticultural Society Garden, Wisley. His recent publications include *The Art of the Botanist* and *The Bulb Book*.